"*Finding Your Heart's Desire* is an amazing look at the struggles we all face in the area of motives. It will give you the practical steps you need to stop seeking the applause of man and begin to live for the glory of God."

Joyce Meyer,
Bible teacher and
bestselling author

"Finally, a book about ambition based on godly principles. R. T. Kendall does it again with his insight into what should motivate us to 'win the gold.'"

Joni Lamb,
co-founder and vice president,
Daystar Television Network;
talk show host and executive producer, *Joni*

"Here is R. T. Kendall in good form: fresh, original, wandering into all the ins and outs of his subject, sometimes provocative, always thought-provoking, sometimes amusing, but always with holiness. Teaching at its best."

Dr. Michael Eaton,
Chrisco Fellowship of Churches; co-pastor,
Chrisco Central Church, Nairobi, Kenya

FINDING
YOUR
HEART'S
DESIRE

FINDING YOUR HEART'S DESIRE

AMBITION, MOTIVATION AND TRUE SUCCESS

R. T. KENDALL

a division of Baker Publishing Group
Minneapolis, Minnesota

248.4 Ken
Ken

Published by Chosen Books
11400 Hampshire Avenue South
Bloomington, Minnesota 55438
www.chosenbooks.com

Chosen Books is a division of
Baker Publishing Group, Grand Rapids, Michigan

Printed in the United States of America

Library of Congress Cataloging-in-Publication Data is on file at the Library of Congress, Washington, DC.

ISBN 978-0-8007-9567-2

Unless otherwise identified, Scripture taken from the HOLY BIBLE, NEW INTERNATIONAL VERSION®. Copyright © 1973, 1978, 1984 Biblica. Used by permission of Zondervan. All rights reserved.

Scripture quotations identified ESV are from The Holy Bible, English Standard Version® (ESV®), copyright © 2001 by Crossway, a publishing ministry of Good News Publishers. Used by permission. All rights reserved. ESV Text Edition: 2007

Scripture quotations identified NEB are from *The New English Bible*. Copyright © 1961, 1970, 1989 by The Delegates of Oxford University Press and The Syndics of the Cambridge University Press. Reprinted by permission.

Scripture quotations identified KJV are from the King James Version of the Bible.

Cover design by Dual Identity, Inc.

13 14 15 16 17 18 19   7 6 5 4 3 2 1

To David and Paul

Contents

Preface

You may think this book is my autobiography. It is, in a sense.

Nearly all of my books are conceived in my mind years before the actual writing. Approximately twenty years ago one of my deacons at Westminster Chapel began saying to me that he hoped I would write a book on the subject of ambition. I cannot say that any bells rang, but I kept his suggestion in mind. Some two or three years ago another deacon from Westminster Chapel said virtually the same thing to me: Would I please consider writing a book on ambition? I find it interesting that two laymen—one a businessman, the other an attorney—would suggest this. I thought of the verse about "two or three witnesses" establishing a matter (Deuteronomy 19:15). From that day this subject began to grow in my mind to the extent that I became gripped. It has been my practice never to proceed with a sermon or a book until I am *gripped*. I have learned—certainly in my case—that the anointing of the Holy Spirit is invariably connected to this phenomenon—being gripped.

It happened that the 2012 Olympics in London were in progress when I began the actual writing of this book. I watched all I could of these thrilling sporting events, including many interviews by Piers Morgan on CNN with people like Sebastian

Coe, Mark Spitz, Michael Phelps and Gabby Douglas. I was enthralled with those occasions and have no doubt been somewhat influenced by them in the writing of this book.

I used to say to David Jermyn, one of the aforementioned deacons, that one day I would dedicate a book to him. I do not think he believed me. But here it is—this one being dedicated to David and also Paul Gardiner, the other deacon who suggested that I write a book on ambition. Both of these unusual and godly men became deacons during the time of my ministry at Westminster Chapel. They both have also been a blessing to Louise and me personally, and I take pleasure in dedicating this book to David and Paul.

My thanks to Jane Campbell, editorial director of Chosen Books, and also to my editor. My friend Lyndon Bowring reads all my manuscripts before they become books, and yet he—and also his wife, Celia—have given me more helpful suggestions this time than for almost any other book I have written. Most of all I thank Louise—my wife of 54 years, my best friend and critic.

R. T. Kendall
Hendersonville, Tennessee
December 2012

Introduction

And I saw that all labor and all achievement spring from man's
envy of his neighbor. This too is meaningless, a chasing after
the wind.

Ecclesiastes 4:4

God uses sex to drive a man to marriage, ambition to drive a
man to service, fear to drive a man to faith.

Martin Luther (1483–1546)

When John F. Kennedy was asked why he wanted to be
president of the United States he replied, "That's where
the power is." Dale Carnegie, the author of *How to Win Friends
and Influence People*, says that the greatest need in people is the
desire to feel important. Psychologist Abraham Maslow says that
the peak experience of a human being is "self-actualization"—
when he or she comes into his or her highest level of self-aware-
ness, or significance.

What is it that gives a person significance? Is it the feeling of
being admired? Is there a significance that goes beyond being

admired or feeling important? If so, how does ambition figure in this need?

It used to make some people smile a little nervously when I quoted the words, "God uses sex to drive a man to marriage, ambition to drive a man to service, fear to drive a man to faith"— especially at weddings. But I almost always quoted it in my wedding sermons (exactly 91 in my 25 years at Westminster Chapel). The congregation usually went quiet for a moment. It helped that I gave Martin Luther the credit for it. I am quite sure it came from Luther. My friend Dr. Michael Eaton says he could not find where Luther said it, although admitting it sounds a lot like Luther. If Martin Luther did not actually say this, someone should have! And if you prove to me that Luther did not coin this phrase, then do forgive me if from now on I should take credit for it myself! In any case, these words lay behind this book in a very significant way.

Definition

Ambition is the *desire to achieve*—often in the eyes of others. Motivation is the driving force that would make it happen. It is the thesis of this book that God often uses ambition to motivate us to do what we need to do—and what He calls us to do. As we shall see in some detail later, ambition is not a virtue; it can be a good thing and also a bad thing. But ambition as a potential for good is one of the main aspects of the human personality that God often taps to motivate us to do His will.

There are exceptions to this, of course. There are people who are motivated to do needed service for other reasons than to be seen of people. There is also a variety of reasons why some people choose to marry. And there are people who may become

Christians without first consciously tasting of the fear of God. But, generally speaking, it is my view that God often motivates us by appealing to our self-interest. The Holy Spirit is the ultimate and final explanation for our conversion and the good we do, yes; but it is nonetheless true that God often motivates us by what sometimes appears as a human explanation.

As for the alleged quote from Luther about sex, ambition and fear, I hasten to point out that these three components in our fallen nature invariably need to be refined. They are transitional: entry points through which God often chooses to get our attention. For example, the *eros* love that lies behind a couple wanting to get married must eventually be upgraded to *agape* love (while not abandoning *eros*) if that marriage is to survive. When husbands are told by the apostle Paul to love their wives as Christ loved the church (see Ephesians 5:25), he did not use *eros* but *agape*.

This is the principle we must grasp when it comes to ambition. The desire to achieve must be upgraded to the degree we get our motivation from wanting to please God alone.

There were at least three Greek words in the ancient Hellenistic world that translate into English as love: (1) *Eros*, physical love, often the only kind of love the world seems to think about, is nonetheless a God-given desire but so often abused; (2) *Philia*, brotherly love, from which we get the name of the great city of Philadelphia, is family love—parent for a child, brother for a sister or a child for a pet; (3) *Agape*, unselfish love, is what motivated God to send His Son into the world. It is the word used by Paul regarding marriage and is the word used throughout 1 Corinthians 13, the famous "love" chapter of the Bible. If, therefore, *eros* love is not soon paralleled by *agape* love in a marriage, that marriage is doomed to fail sooner or later. The folly of the present generation is that too many people marry for *eros* love then wonder why after a few months they are so unhappy. Seven marriages for Elizabeth Taylor did not bring her happiness.

If, therefore, God uses ambition to drive a man or woman to service, such a motivation must develop so that it becomes God-oriented. This means that a love for the glory of God must eclipse that natural ambition, which originally set a person on a path to achieve. Sadly the ancient Pharisees' desire to do good works only to be seen of men (see Matthew 6:1ff) never matured. You could say that the Pharisees never grew up. Their lack of maturity also became their downfall, this being the very reason they missed their Messiah.

Fear As a Motivation

When the hymn writer John Newton injected that second verse into his great hymn "Amazing Grace"—"'Twas grace that taught my heart to fear," he was no doubt partly referring to his own experience. And yet this kind of thinking was axiomatic in his tradition. Martin Luther taught that we must know God as an enemy before we can know Him as a friend. It was an assumption in the theology of the reformers (as in Luther and John Calvin—and later by Jonathan Edwards) that the preaching of the wrath and justice of God would lead people to repentance. After all, the earliest message of the New Testament was that of John the Baptist warning people to "flee from the wrath to come" (Matthew 3:7 KJV).

There is no doubt that I myself was convicted of my sins by the awareness of God's wrath; therefore, fear initially motivated me to be saved. But I suspect that so little preaching is done nowadays along that line that, if fear must necessarily set in before one has faith, few would be saved! This is partly why I said there are exceptions. There are many ways God may use to bring His people to salvation. That said, for those who do come to Christ out of a fear of God's wrath, such anxiety and trepidation must—without ever losing a sense of a healthy fear of God—grow into a sweet intimacy with the Holy Spirit. This comes through an ever-increasing knowledge of Jesus Christ through prayer, reading the Bible, good teaching and walking in the light. The result will be to experience the loving fellowship of the Father (see 1 John 1:7).

Funnily enough, the quote from Ecclesiastes 4:4, presumably written by Solomon, is more controversial than the alleged Luther quote: *All labor and achievement spring from man's envy of his neighbor.* Really? "All" labor? "All" achievement? Luther may have his opinion, but Ecclesiastes 4:4 is from Holy Scripture—the infallible Word of God. Or is that verse there merely to show Solomon's personal opinion based upon his own observations?

There are at least two interpretations of Ecclesiastes 4:4, both of which are valid. First, that it is saying how people would not be motivated to get things done or to achieve any measure of success were it not for the good feeling we get from *making other people jealous!* If people will not discover or admire what I achieve, then what's the point?

"Iron sharpens iron" (Proverbs 27:17). Perhaps the greatest rivalry of recent years is that of Bill Gates—one of the world's wealthiest men—associated with Microsoft, and the late Steve Jobs, associated with Apple. Steve Jobs once said that Bill Gates never had an original thought in his life! Jobs, too, amassed great personal wealth. He said that when he was 23 he was worth one million dollars, ten million when he was 24 and one hundred million when he was 25. He also said that he is the only person to have lost a quarter of a billion in one year. And yet he eventually did what was unprecedented, rescuing Apple from a major setback and making it the richest company in the world. When I use my MacBook Air to write this book I think of Ecclesiastes 4:4 and the rivalry of Gates and Jobs.

But the second interpretation of Ecclesiastes 4:4 shows how achievement springs from the desire to *do one better* than what has been done. This motivation refers not so much to making others jealous but believing I can do one better—whether or not they know it. In other words: *one-upmanship*. It is the stuff of which Olympic gold medalists are made. But does "all" achievement spring from the desire to outdo what has been done? Either interpretation of Ecclesiastes 4:4, in any case, shows how ambition motivates a person to service or success.

Albert Einstein (1879–1955) was one of the greatest intellects of modern times, arguably the greatest mind in five hundred years. Who would have thought that such a genius would ever need to approach life with the thought of being ambitious? With a brain like that you might think that ambition would surely not even come into the picture. And yet Einstein said, "You have to learn the rules of the game. And then you have to play better than anyone else." Imagine Einstein saying that!

There are basically two words for ambition in the New Testament—one showing it can be a good thing, the other an evil thing. The Greek word *philotimeomai* (etymologically "love honor"), which shows that ambition can be a good thing, literally translates as "aspire to a goal" or have ambition. Using this word, Paul revealed something very interesting about himself: "It has always been my ambition to preach the gospel where Christ was not known, so that I would not be building on someone else's foundation" (Romans 15:20). He used the word in 2 Corinthians 5:9: "So we make it our goal to please him"—the noblest ambition a person can have. Hence the New English Bible translates it: "We therefore make it our ambition, wherever we are, here or there, to be acceptable to him." Paul used the same word in urging the Thessalonians: "Make it your ambition to lead a quiet life, to mind your own business and to work with your hands" (1 Thessalonians 4:11). The other Greek word is *eritheia*, meaning a "base self-seeking," or simply "baseness." Hence it is always used in a negative sense: "self-seeking" (Romans 2:8) or "selfish ambition" (Galatians 5:20; Philippians 1:17; 2:3; James 3:14, 16).

Seven Purposes of this Book

What is the purpose of writing this book? First and foremost, I hope to motivate every reader to experience the joy and praise that comes from God alone—without caring whether people know what you may have achieved or sought to accomplish. That is the highest joy that can come to us this side of our going to heaven.

Second, I hope this book will teach us to become aware of our motives. We all tend to play games with ourselves—and others—never examining why we do this or that.

Third, this book should bring us to the place where we may have a greater measure of objectivity about ourselves. That would mean—at least in part—seeing our motives in a particular way and knowing *why* we do what we do.

Fourth, I hope this book will teach us how to think. Dr. Martyn Lloyd-Jones used to say that the Christian faith ought to teach a person how to think.

Fifth, this book is written also to teach us patience with others. "Every person is worth understanding," says Clyde Narramore. This book should provide a caution against judging people too quickly or harshly.

Sixth, I want to encourage you to use whatever motivation or ambition that lies within you to channel it in the direction of pleasing God. Whatever level of motivation you have, seize upon it with the view of obtaining the glory and honor that comes from God and not people.

Finally, I pray that this book will motivate you to come into God's inheritance for your life here below and that you will be among those who receive a reward at the Judgment Seat of Christ. If this book should be the means to make that happen I would be overjoyed.

Don't Just Stand There— Do Something!

Everyone who competes in the games goes into strict training. They do it to get a crown that will not last; but we do it to get a crown that will last forever.

1 Corinthians 9:25

I can't stand losing.

Mark Spitz,
winner of seven Olympic gold medals

If you want to be the best, you have to do what others are not willing to do.

Michael Phelps,
winner of 22 Olympic gold medals

How can ye believe, which receive honour one of another, and seek not the honour that cometh from God only?

John 5:44 KJV

If ambition is the desire to achieve, often in the eyes of others, motivation is the fuel that drives a person to achieve that ambition. Ambition is the dream; motivation gets things done, the latter being the difference between waking up before dawn to pound the pavement instead of lazing at home all day.

The apostle Paul was a highly motivated and ambitious man. He wanted the "prize," the "crown"—referring not to salvation or heaven but the reward that will be given at the Judgment Seat of Christ. "For we must all appear before the judgment seat of Christ, that each one may receive what is due him for the things done while in the body, whether good or bad" (2 Corinthians 5:10). Paul made a definite and very important distinction between salvation—guaranteeing heaven—and achieving an inheritance *on the way* to heaven.

Every Christian is called to receive an inheritance. This comes through faith and obedience. It begins at conversion and culminates at the Judgment Seat of Christ. We come into our inheritance here below as we walk in the light. The result of obedience is to discover and fulfill God's will and plan for your life. I wish I could say that all Christians automatically come into their inheritances. But no. Some Christians do indeed come into their inheritances; others (sadly) blow it and never enjoy or realize what was rightfully theirs. The ultimate purpose of one's inheritance, however, is to receive a reward at the Judgment Seat of Christ. I wish I could say that all Christians equally and inevitably receive a reward at the Judgment Seat of Christ. Some will, some won't. Whether you or I will receive a reward will be unveiled when we openly receive what is *due* for the things done in the body, "whether good or bad."

I have heard some Christians say, "I don't care whether or not I receive a reward at the Judgment Seat of Christ, I just want to make it to heaven." I reply: "You may feel that way now, but you won't feel that way then."

Two Great Awakenings

You may have heard of the Cane Ridge Revival (at its height in the early 1800s), called "America's Second Great Awakening." One Sunday morning a Methodist lay preacher stood on a fallen tree to address some fifteen thousand people in an area called Cane Ridge in Bourbon County, Kentucky. These people came in their covered wagons from several adjoining states for fellowship, prayer and Bible teaching, this being the beginning of the "camp meeting" phenomenon. The preacher took his text from 2 Corinthians 5:10, that we must all stand before the Judgment Seat of Christ to give an account of the things done in the body, whether good or bad. As he spoke people began to fall involuntarily to the ground, lying motionless for hours—but getting up after a few hours with great assurance of salvation. Others fell to the ground. Between that Sunday morning and the following Wednesday there were never fewer than five hundred people prostrate on the ground under the power of the Holy Spirit. They called it the "sound of Niagara," as people could hear the roar of their shouts a mile away.

You more likely may have heard of the first Great Awakening in the eighteenth century, peaking around 1741 when Jonathan Edwards took his text from Deuteronomy 32:35: "Their foot shall slide in due time" (KJV). When he finished preaching many listeners were in fear of going to hell. People in the church held on to pews to keep from sliding into hell; strong men were seen holding on to tree trunks outside to keep from sliding into hell. It was an unforgettable event, a word that spread all over New

England in days and across the Atlantic into England in weeks. The reason for there being a Bible Belt in America is traceable largely to the preaching of Jonathan Edwards and the Cane Ridge Revival.

These two great awakenings have in common the assumption of life beyond the grave and the Final Judgment. It is not often in Church history—that is, since Pentecost—when there was such a demonstration of the immediate and direct power of the Holy Spirit. Talk about motivation! When people are holding on to pews or tree trunks to keep from going to hell, no further human persuasion that I know of is needed. It was a display of the raw power of God, the sheer work of the Spirit. It may be presumed that the fear of God lay at the bottom of both awakenings. As for the Judgment Seat of Christ, Paul followed his reference to it with these words: "Knowing therefore the terror of the Lord, we persuade men" (2 Corinthians 5:11 KJV). I would only add that the obvious manifestation of the Holy Spirit upon the two aforementioned events suggests a pretty strong hint of God's approval upon the content of the preaching that preceded and precipitated these astonishing phenomena. Both refer to eschatology (doctrine of last things) and imply motivation by the fear of God.

But in the absence of such immediate and direct power from the Throne of Grace, what does one do to get people motivated? Having referred to the fear of God as a motivation (see 2 Corinthians 5:11), Paul in three verses later said, "Christ's love compels us" (2 Corinthians 5:14). Some might call Paul's language contradictory: motivation by fear and then love. I reply: Both are true. It is love that compels us to warn people of coming judgment. The kindest questions you can put to anybody are: Where will you be one hundred years from now? Do you know for sure that if you were to die today, you would go to heaven? And if you were to stand before God (and you will) and He were to ask you (and He might), "Why should I let you into My heaven?" what would you say? It is the fear of God that should compel us to warn people; it is because of our love for them that we warn them.

Personal Testimony

I was converted at the age of six, kneeling at my parents' bedside on Easter Sunday—April 5, 1942. The kind of preaching I heard in those days and the kind of Christianity into which I was born were permeated with an atmosphere of the fear of God and the reality of heaven or hell when you die. I have often wondered if my Nazarene church in Ashland, Kentucky—located about a hundred miles from Cane Ridge—was possibly at the end of the momentum of that historic revival begun over a century before. There is no doubt that my perception of the Christian faith was shaped by this kind of theology.

I will be talking some about my dad in this book. My father was a godly man. But, for better or for worse, he drove me to a need to achieve that, probably, gave me a double dose of ambition. From childhood I have wanted to be the best at what I did; coming short of being the very best made me very frustrated, if not angry. When John McEnroe, to whom I shall refer again below, played tennis at Wimbledon—often shouting to the umpire—I always sympathized. That's me. John McEnroe's father drove him to be the very best. In my case, my dad (without meaning to) also made me feel I never quite came up to his lofty standard. When I got a report card, which had to be signed by a parent, he would not sign it unless I got As and Bs. If I got a C or D he would have my mother sign it. But even when I got straight As, which I did sometimes, he always mediated the impression that those As could be A-pluses if I worked harder. I recall watching a home movie with me cutting the grass in our yard and seeing my dad motioning me to be sure I did not miss any tall grass! He arranged for me to sell *Grit* magazine to the neighbors at the age of ten. When I was twelve he gave me a bicycle so I could earn money as a newspaper boy. I got up at five a.m. every morning before I went to school to deliver the *Cincinnati Enquirer* to a wider section of Ashland. When I was fifteen I delivered the *Ashland Daily Independent* after school to about 120 homes.

When I was ten, having been an A student for years, my schoolwork fell; I started making only Bs and Cs. I felt my teacher did not like me for some reason and I never made As again. She told my parents, "I don't think R. T. is an A student"—which made an indelible impression on me, making me feel it was no use to try after that. In my senior year at high school I failed at algebra. I played on the basketball team in junior high, but when I failed to make the first string (as we called it), I turned to music—learning how to play the oboe. I wanted to be the best at something. I did fairly well at this, was even given a scholarship in a Kentucky university, but I did not want that as a career.

While in high school I became a member of the debate team. I developed an interest in world affairs, debating whether the Atlantic Pact nations should form a federal union. This led me to meet Senator John Sherman Cooper of Kentucky. He did something nice for me when I was in Washington, D.C., taking me into the vice president's office and inviting me to sit in his chair. "Make a wish," I was told as I sat there. For some reason, sitting in the chair of the vice president of the United States, I bowed my head and said, "Lord, make me a great soul winner."

In the autumn of 1953 I entered Trevecca Nazarene College (now University). I used to think I wanted to be a trial lawyer, but in 1954 felt the call of God on me to preach. Three months later at the age of nineteen I became the pastor of the Palmer, Tennessee, Church of the Nazarene, traveling there on weekends and keeping up my studies at Trevecca. One Monday morning—October 31, 1955—while driving in my car, I had an experience that was to change my life forever. The glory of the Lord filled the car.

There as I drove on old U.S. 41 at about 6:30 a.m. the Lord Jesus appeared alongside me, making intercession for me. Although this was no doubt a spiritual experience, it was as real as if it were physical and before my very eyes. An hour later, hearing the words of Jesus to the Father, "He wants it," the reply came: "He can have it." I have queried for years what "it" was; I do know that at that moment I entered in to a rest of soul and peace that I did not know was possible on this earth. By the time I arrived in Nashville I knew I was eternally saved. By the end of that day I began to believe in predestination. I wondered if I was discovering something new. For several months the person of Jesus was literally as real to me as anybody around me. During those months I had about a dozen visions. It became clear to me from them that God was going to use me—even internationally and outside my old denomination.

In 1956, having hastily decided to leave Trevecca and launch out immediately into an evangelistic preaching ministry, I encountered an immediate, abrupt and humiliating failure. I began to take myself too seriously. As I tell in my book *The Anointing*, after buying a tent that seated two thousand people, and holding nightly services near Ashland, we closed the "revival" in some three weeks. The highest attendance was about thirty people. My dear dad accused me of breaking with God and departing from the faith of my old denomination. Trying my best to impress him, I foolishly assured him I would be in a huge ministry within a year from that date. Some of those visions convinced me I would even have an international ministry. A year later I was not preaching at all. Five years later I was selling vacuum cleaners door to door to make a living. I had nothing whatever to show my father that I was in God's will.

Despite the great sense of God I had experienced in 1955–1956, I obviously made several huge mistakes. Among them included my being defensive about the experience that happened to me when driving in my car that October morning. I began to care too much what my friends thought of me. The opinions of my peers began to govern my motives. I longed for vindication—in their eyes, not to mention my dad's. I also went deeply into debt, which became one of the reasons I could not enter into a full-time Christian ministry for years. In the meantime, that great sense of God also diminished.

John 5:44

But not all was folly in those days. Perhaps the most important discovery in 1956—if not my entire life—was coming across John 5:44. I cannot explain why it meant so much to me, I only know that this verse was somehow implanted in my spirit so definitely and deeply that fulfilling it, more than any other verse in the Bible that I am aware of, eventually became my greatest ambition. I am *so* thankful to God that it gripped me. In ever-increasing measure, John 5:44 became the verse that I sought to be governed by. Not that I always did this. If only. But the New International Version (emphasis added) translates it: "How can you believe if you accept praise from one another, yet *make no effort* to obtain the praise that comes from the only God?" Whereas the King James Version (the only version I used in those days) says "seek," the NIV says "make no effort," which I found helpful. We are not judged by whether we are completely successful but whether we sincerely *make an effort* to obtain the praise that comes from God alone. Most translations say "the only God." This is no doubt right.

I will admit, however, I am glad that the KJV says "God only" because it seemed to set in bold relief that it was the opinion and praise of *God alone* that mattered, not the opinion and praise of people. The reason that the Jews missed their Messiah was that they only cared about the praise and honor that came from one another. The notion of receiving the honor that would come from God alone was not remotely on their radar screen. So Jesus asked them a question, "How *can* you believe, if you receive praise from one another and make no attempt to receive the praise from the only God?" The reason they were *unable* to believe was because they not only lived for the admiration of people but *made no attempt* to receive the praise that would come from God alone.

This verse continues to be relevant to all of us today. Jonathan Edwards taught us that the task of every generation is to discover in which direction the Sovereign Redeemer is moving, then move in that direction. But how can we *know* in which direction our Lord God is moving? Answer: only in proportion to how much we make an effort to obtain the praise that comes from God alone. In other words, God can be at work before our very eyes and we can miss what He is doing as the Pharisees missed their Messiah.

Here is another reason why John 5:44 is so wonderful—for you and me: It sets us free to be the best at something without competing with each other, and looking over our shoulders at others in the race. I just finished watching the London Olympics. The man who easily won the gold medal in the marathon coasted to the finish line while looking back at his nearest opponent with glee. Paul said that we are "in a race"—very possibly referring to the Olympics or its equivalent; "all the runners run, but only one gets the prize": that is, the gold. Paul then added, "Run in such a way as to get the prize" (1 Corinthians 9:24). The prize he was referring to was the "crown"—the reward or prize—to be handed out at the Judgment Seat of Christ. This is why he closed that section with these words: "I beat my body and make it my slave so that after I have preached to others, I myself will not be disqualified for the prize" (1 Corinthians 9:27). Paul was not referring to his personal salvation—which was not in question. What he wanted was the reward of his inheritance at the Judgment Seat of Christ.

All of Us Can Win the Gold

Here is the crucial point. When it comes to the Olympics, all the athletes are in competition with each other. But when it comes to pleasing God—which is the *only* way you get your reward—*all can win the gold*. We are not in competition with each other. Here is why: God chose our inheritance for us (see Psalm 47:4). Your inheritance is not mine; mine is not yours. Each of us has a unique inheritance. All I have to do is come into that inheritance here on earth—then receive the prize at the Judgment Seat of Christ. You and I are therefore not in competition with each other. We can encourage each other to win the gold! In fact, my effort to encourage you helps me to win! Your encouraging me to press on helps you!

But it comes with effort. I heard Michael Phelps say to Piers Morgan on CNN that he had been in the pool swimming and training *every single day for the previous five years* in preparation for the 2012 London Olympics. Imagine dedication like that! The apostle Paul knew something of the ancient Olympics. "Everyone who competes in the games goes into strict training" (1 Corinthians 9:25). The ambition to win the gold must be matched by motivation to undergo the most diligent kind of training. Why do they do it? "To get a crown that will not last" (verse 25). Their moment of glory, putting on the gold medal and showing it for their remaining years on earth, is at best temporary. But to receive God's praise and honor at the Judgment Seat of Christ is to wear a crown that will last throughout eternity.

As I said above, I was driven as a boy to want to be the best at what I did. When I was not the best in my class back in Ashland, I turned to basketball. When I did not make the first string, I turned to playing the oboe. When I went into the ministry I wanted to be the best preacher. When I finished Oxford I wanted to be the best theologian. Some of my critics said I was educated beyond my intelligence. That hurt a bit, but only because I feared they could be right. But whatever goals I had in early days at Westminster Chapel, my ambitions, plans and wishes "at His feet in ashes lay," as the hymn put it. Through the influence of Arthur Blessitt, who has carried a cross around the world, I was smitten with God's overwhelming call on my life to make evangelism a priority. I began our Pilot Light ministry, witnessing on the streets of Victoria between the Houses of Parliament and Buckingham Palace. I sought to do this during my last twenty years at Westminster Chapel. Many were led to Jesus Christ during those years, making me wonder if God was answering my prayer prayed in the chair of the vice president of

the United States. I have no doubt that my ambition and drivenness from my father's influence and childhood experiences played
no small part in my efforts to make things happen in those days.

If motivation were sufficient to accomplish my goals, believe
me, they would have been achieved. My vain and selfish ambition
to fill Westminster Chapel from top to bottom was matched by
enough motivation to fill Wembley Stadium. But God chose to
humble me to dust instead. Mercifully my ambition eventually
matured to focusing on God's honor alone. And what had been
a carnal desire to prove myself was transcended by a determination to practice total forgiveness, dignifying trials and keeping
my eyes on Jesus.

Jesus gave us a sobering parable about those who bury their
talents as opposed to making them earn interest (kindly see
my book *The Parables of Jesus*). The Parable of the Talents
is essentially about coming into your inheritance as opposed
to forfeiting it—so needlessly. Those with five or two talents
doubled their inheritance while the man with one talent foolishly hid his talent in the ground, justifying himself for doing
so. The result was that he lost everything—his one talent and
any reward he could have had received (Matthew 25:14–30).

Ambition matters. Motivation matters. Training matters.
Preparation matters. But these must be sprinkled by the blood
of Jesus Christ and immersed in the Holy Spirit. And if five
years of daily swimming culminates in a total of 22 gold medals for one of the greatest athletes of all time, how much more
will a life of faith and obedience result in the greatest joy and
honor of all: that which comes only from God? It is when the
Lord Jesus Himself looks at us straight into our eyes and says,
"Well done." It is as if Jesus will say to us, "Congratulations."
It doesn't get better than that. It is worth pursuing.

Developing a Godly Ambition

He chose our inheritance for us.

Psalm 47:4

So then, just as you received Christ Jesus as Lord, continue to live in him, rooted and built up in him, strengthened in the faith as you were taught, and overflowing with thankfulness.

Colossians 2:6–7

Take heed that you faithfully perform the business you have to do in the world, from a response to the commands of God; and not from an ambitious desire of being esteemed better than others.

David Brainerd (1718–1747)

The worst thing that can happen to a man is to succeed before he is ready.

Martyn Lloyd-Jones (1899–1981)

Try to imagine for a moment that you are a well-known minister who can be seen on YouTube. Let us suppose people have admired you for years. Let us say that you became an overnight sensation when praying for the sick years ago. Let us even agree that you were sovereignly raised up by God and given an anointing by Him to perform many undoubted miracles and healings. But what if this same anointing apparently began to diminish after a few years and finally lifted almost entirely? If so, we might reasonably wonder whether: (1) God sovereignly withdrew this anointing from you; or (2) you forfeited this anointing for avoidable reasons. You remained sexually pure and your life would *not* end in disgrace. The latter part of your life, however, was characterized by considerable success and prestige but—some think—sadly mixed with questionable wisdom. The healing anointing that you once had, in any case, apparently never returned.

What if we now imagine a different scenario. You are a well-known TV evangelist who was reaching millions through effective preaching. Your preaching was powerful and did great good in leading souls to Christ throughout the world. But through sexual misconduct you were found out and, consequently, lost most of your following. Though you can still be seen on television, your influence is a mere shadow of what it was. How would you explain the irony that your effectiveness as a preacher never actually diminished? In other words, your sexual immorality did not militate against your powerful oratory. Had you not gotten caught, would you have continued on and on as if you were sexually pure? Is it that your gift functioned because the gifts and callings of God are irrevocable (see Romans 11:29)? Could this explain how King Saul could prophesy while trying to kill young David (see 1 Samuel 19:23–24)?

The purpose of this chapter is to show the importance of having a healthy ambition to pursue God's will for us. To those of us who may have been given a huge dose of ambition, we must be challenged to channel that ambition for God's glory—the pursuit of integrity, holiness and finishing well. God often uses ambition to drive us to service and success; Satan uses unsanctified ambition to destroy us.

The Modesto Manifesto

Consider now a person who has remained above reproach in his life and ministry—Billy Graham. He is in a category quite apart from either scenario above. Although I never had the privilege of being close to him, I have spent some time with him so that I feel as though I know him a little bit.

His song leader, Cliff Barrows, kindly told me about a commitment to God that Billy made many years ago to be financially and sexually pure. Indeed, Billy Graham, Cliff and Billie Barrows, Grady Wilson and George Beverly Shea entered into a covenant together in Modesto, California, in 1948. Cliff said, "Billy was concerned about the fictional character of the Elmer Gantry image that was developing toward traveling evangelists. He wanted to avoid the recurring problem that many evangelists seem to have." This group came up with four core values: (1) *humility*: never criticize local pastors or churches or have an anti-clergy attitude; (2) *accountability*: avoid financial abuses and have, in place, accountability for funds collected and expenditures; (3) *integrity*: in publicity and reporting, never claim higher attendance numbers or exaggerate successes (decisions for Christ) that could not be documented—always giving God glory for His work; (4) *purity*: avoid any situation that would bring the appearance of immorality, compromise or suspicion. This became known as the Modesto Manifesto since it was born in Cliff's hometown in California. Calling it that "would help us to remember it," Cliff said. "Many situations occurred in the years that followed where they were brought to mind. Bev Shea and I have been with him sixty-seven years!"

When I think of Dr. Martyn Lloyd-Jones's observation that the "worst thing that can happen to a man is to succeed before he is ready," it seems to me that Billy Graham is an exception to that principle. Billy had great success when he was young—and has lived with unparalleled fame (being a friend of presidents and royalty) for the whole of his life. Although he, like all great servants of God, has been an ambitious man, God has preserved him from any scandal. Billy has kept himself financially and sexually pure. To put it another way, it seems to me that Billy Graham, like King David, has come into a most pleasant inheritance (Psalm16:6)—and has not blown it away.

But now will you try to imagine a third scenario: that you are a successful and famous evangelist. Will you receive a greater reward at the Judgment Seat of Christ? What if the following axiom is true: "The greater the profile below, the less in heaven"? Is it not true that at the Judgment Seat of Christ the rewards will be given to all the saved without regard to their earthly fame? The rewards will, therefore, be given to the known and unknown—and only with regard to their faithfulness and obedience. Do not be surprised, then, that the greater rewards will be given to those who were unknown but faithful—with no earthly profile, no applause, no accolades and no recognition. But these same people who have suffered while maintaining integrity, dignifying trials, totally forgiving those who hurt them, demonstrating thankfulness without grumbling and upholding the honor and glory of God will be those at the head of the queue to receive Christ's "Well done." Those of us who have had a measure of recognition here on earth have *already* been largely rewarded. God will decide what else might be coming to such people. In a word: I will not be surprised that the less profile below, the more there; the more recognition below, the less at the Judgment Seat of Christ.

Inheritance

Every Christian has been called to come into his or her inheritance. This is the next step forward for any convert. It is put by Paul like this: "Just as you received Christ Jesus the Lord, *continue* to live in him" (Colossians 2:6, emphasis added). God does not say to us at conversion, "Glad to meet you, see you in heaven," as if there were no further relationship with Him until we are in glory. No. We are called to enter into our inheritance. This is obtained by walking in holiness, gratitude and openness to the internal testimony of the Holy Spirit. This kind of guidance is promised to each of us when Paul said that "God will make clear" to us what we need to know regarding His will (Philippians 3:15). He does this by His Word—the Bible—and by the inner testimony of the Spirit. When we walk in the light we experience fellowship with the Father and the cleansing of the blood of Jesus Christ (see 1 John 1:7).

The word *inheritance* may be used interchangeably with *reward*, *crown* or *prize*. See Colossians 3:24 where *inheritance* is actually called a reward.

Here is the premise: All who are saved will go to heaven, but not all who go to heaven receive a reward (prize, crown, inheritance) at the Judgment Seat of Christ. It is there we receive a reward for the deeds done "while in the body" (2 Corinthians 5:10), that is, how we respond to God's Word *after* our conversion and before we die. In the light of our being saved we are to present our "bodies as living sacrifices, holy and pleasing to God" (Romans 12:1). Those who live lives pleasing to God come into their inheritance below and receive the culmination of that inheritance above, namely, a reward at the Judgment Seat of Christ. Those who do not live lives pleasing to God will "suffer loss" of reward but "will be saved, but only as one escaping through the flames" (1 Corinthians 3:15). You cannot lose your salvation, but you *can* blow away your inheritance and forfeit a reward at the Judgment Seat of Christ.

If I have been influenced by John 5:44, as described earlier, I should add that I have been equally motivated by the Judgment Seat of Christ. This truth—so sobering—has been a major factor in my wanting to live a holy life, to exemplify John 5:44 and please the Lord. It is at the Judgment Seat of Christ that not only will I receive a reward if I finish well, but you, too, will actually witness this. Yes, you will see with your own eyes and hear with your own ears what Jesus says to me and about me on that awesome occasion. This is the scary part. It would be nice if the Judgment Seat of Christ were absolutely private and personal—that no one else could look in on to observe what I will receive (or forfeit). But no. You will hear what Jesus Christ says to me and I will hear what He says to *you*. Like it or not, that is the way it is. "There is nothing hidden that will not be disclosed, and nothing concealed that will not be known or brought out into the open" (Luke 8:17).

But will sins washed away by the blood of Christ be exposed? No. I actually deal with this in some detail in my book *God Gives Second Chances* (called *Second Chance* in the U.K.). It is my belief that those sins that have been cleansed—and for which I have been granted repentance—will not be known or exposed at the Judgment Seat of Christ. We can thank God for that. But all unconfessed sin will be faced by us. It is surely enough to make us cautious, conscientious and careful to heed all the admonitions in Scripture as to how to live the Christian life. In other words, not only will I stand before God, but I will do this with all watching me.

There are two good reasons, then, to walk in Christ as we received Him: (1) to come into our inheritance here on earth; and (2) to receive—and not forfeit—a reward at the Judgment Seat of Christ.

Two Ways of Perceiving Inheritance

Our inheritance below is to be understood two ways: internal and external.

The internal inheritance is the immediate and direct witness of the Holy Spirit. It is referred to more than one way in Scripture—e.g., entering God's rest; full assurance; fellowship with the Father. It comes down to *intimacy* with God. It is the reward below given by the Spirit for walking in the light and pleasing God. The external inheritance refers to the way God rewards us outwardly here below. For example, I am called to be a Bible teacher and preacher. I could not have known on April 5, 1942, that one day I would become the minister of Westminster Chapel, even to be an author of some books. I could not have known that I would marry Louise—the loveliest girl on earth—or that I would be the father of two wonderful children. These are examples of *external* inheritance. With that said I must add that any external inheritance that has come to me is the consequence of the sheer grace and mercy of God. I have let God down so often that—were you to know the truth—you would say, "If God could use R. T. He could use anybody." Believe me, this is the truth. I wrote *God Gives Second Chances* out of personal experience.

One's internal inheritance comes by taking seriously the rewards and warnings in Scripture, by putting God first in one's life, by obeying the impulses of the Holy Spirit, by upholding doctrines that may or may not have been well received, by dignifying trials, by tithing one's income, by practicing total forgiveness and being unashamed of Christ in the world. These matters pertain to one's inner walk with God. But there is more: Such people will have enjoyed sweet peace, an inner witness to what grieves or pleases the Spirit, insight into Scripture and God's kind sense of conveying to them that they are pleasing Him. These, then, are examples of the *internal* inheritance.

Caution: *The internal must go before the external.* In other words, it is not my job to figure out what God will do with my life. That's *His* job. Don't ask, What will my external inheritance be? Ask, Am I walking in the light of God? My task is to obey His word; His responsibility is opening and closing doors.

The Sovereignty of God

Now here is the crucial point: *God chooses our inheritance for us* (see Psalm 47:4). We do not decide this. He does. He is sovereign. This is best illustrated by the way Israel's inheritance was decided. There were twelve tribes. Each tribe was given a section of the land. Each one's territory was chosen by lot (see Numbers 26:52–56). Call it drawing straws, rolling the dice—whatever. The point is, it was *out of their hands*. God decided.

This is the way it is with every child of God—with each of us—as well; God decides what our lot or inheritance is. So King David could say, "The boundary lines have fallen for me in pleasant places; surely I have a delightful inheritance" (Psalm 16:6). You might (perhaps cynically) say, "Quite. David *would* say that, wouldn't he? After all, he was king." I reply: So, too, each of us—you and I—if we will walk in the light God gives us, we *also* will say, "Surely I have a delightful inheritance." There will be no need to look over the shoulder and say as Peter did about John, "What about him?" (John 21:21). Peter was put in his place quickly (see verse 22) as we, too, will be when we begin looking over our shoulders at another's inheritance and not what God has specifically chosen for us!

To put it another way: God has decided beforehand our callings, our anointing, our capacity to grasp His will, our measure of grace, our gifts and our places in His Kingdom. *We will not miss* what He has in mind for us if we are faithful to follow Him, walk in Him and keep our eyes on Him. But remember: the internal first, then the external. In other words, do not ask, "Will I be another Billy Graham? Will I be famous? Will I get married? Will I be secure?" Ask instead, "Lord, what do You want me to do?" Follow Him. He will visit you, witness to you, make Himself real to you. And when the internal is actualized (to use Abraham Maslow's phrase), you will be *happy* with the external calling God has set out for you.

The late John Stott died at the age of ninety. He was one of the most saintly men I have known. And yet, only months before he died he asked my friend Lyndon Bowring, "Please pray that I will finish well." Billy Graham is finishing well. I want to end well. I am not there yet. I am taking nothing for granted. "The heart is deceitful above all things, and desperately wicked

(Jeremiah 17:9 KJV). I am in Paul's mindset when he wrote, "I beat my body and make it my slave so that after I have preached to others, I myself will not be disqualified for the prize" (1 Corinthians 9:27). This was in AD 55. But some ten years later Paul felt more confident. While waiting to be summoned to his death at any moment he said, "I have fought the good fight. I have finished the race, I have kept the faith. Now there is in store for me the crown of righteousness, which the Lord, the righteous Judge, will award to me on that day" (2 Timothy 4:7–8). A reward—crown, prize—was very important to Paul. That to me speaks volumes. I do not mean to be unfair, but I never felt it was a mark of spirituality to say, "I don't care about a reward, I just want to make it to heaven." Paul did not think like this.

Suppose you are perceived as a disgraced evangelist or fallen leader. None of us is your judge. But if indeed you have somehow gotten off the rails, how do you think it happened? No one knows, of course, what is going on inwardly or if you have repented since you apparently let God down. Have you asked how the fall happened or how it started? Had you begun to take yourself a bit seriously—or encouraged and welcomed applause too quickly? Were you too careless with the opposite sex? Did you begin to be less than discreet with finances?

The things "done while in the body, whether good or bad" (2 Corinthians 5:10) pertain largely to money, sex and power. How we behave "while" in the body with regard to these three important matters will almost certainly determine whether we receive a reward at the Judgment Seat of Christ or whether we lose that reward and are saved by fire (see 1 Corinthians 3:15).

I am an ambitious man. I also want a reward at the Judgment Seat of Christ. I want to be faithful to the end. I am determined—by God's grace—to channel that ambition toward pleasing God as long as I have breath. I want to hear Jesus say to me, "Well done." Don't you, too? Then let's be sure we grasp the next step forward—pursuing our inheritance—that we do not come short of what has been chosen for us. The fact that an inheritance has been chosen for us does not mean we will automatically come into it. Every tribe of Israel had to fight and conquer the land before them. Paul called it "the good fight." We can all win. We can all win the prize. We are not in competition with each other. We all can equally please the Lord.

God Stoops to Our Level

"Do not judge, and you will not be judged. Do not condemn, and you will not be condemned. Forgive, and you will be forgiven. Give, and it will be given to you. . . . For with the measure you use, it will be measured to you."

Luke 6:37–38

Remember this: Whoever sows sparingly will also reap sparingly, and whoever sows generously will also reap generously. . . . You will be made rich in every way.

2 Corinthians 9:6, 11

Men are moved by two levers only: fear and self-interest.

Napoleon Bonaparte (1769–1821)

Will springs from two elements: of moral sense and self-interest.

Abraham Lincoln (1809–1865)

I never cease to be amazed that one of the most tender ways of God is that He looks for an *entry point in us* by which He can motivate us to obedience. Yes, He stoops to our weakness, reaches us where we are—even appealing to our self-interest to get us to do what we ought to do anyway!

Jesus told us not to be judgmental. Do *you* like being judged? I do not. I find it hurtful. Jesus told us how to avoid the discomfort of being judged: "Do not judge, and *you* will not be judged." Do you like being condemned by someone? Then "do not condemn, and *you* will not be condemned" (Luke 6:37, emphasis added). One of the ways to avoid the pain of someone pointing a finger at you—or keeping a record of your wrongs—is for *you* not to point the finger at others in the first place or keep a record of their wrongs.

Jesus, therefore, appeals to our self-interest—our very feelings, aspirations and sense of well-being—when applying truth to us that we ought to uphold and carry out in the first place! In other words, Jesus could have said, "Do not judge, do not condemn"—full stop. Period. End of story. Nothing more. He could have said, "Keep this command because I said it." But He did not do that; He gave us more, showing that it is in our own interest not to judge or condemn.

This is a consistent pattern of the God of the Bible that many of us overlook. Too many of us (and I do include myself) have perceived God as harsh, hard, strict and having a take-it-or-leave-it attitude. That is not the complete picture of the God of the Old Testament. It is not the God of the New Testament. It is not Jesus. It is not the God and Father of our Lord Jesus Christ. The God of the Bible is loving, merciful, tender and kind. He knows our frame and remembers that we are "dust" (Psalm 103:14). Our Great High Priest is touched with the feeling of our weaknesses (see Hebrews 4:15). What a wonderful Lord and Savior we have!

God not only motivates us to do His will by showing us *why* we should obey Him; He even supplies the grace to carry out His command. St. Augustine (354–430) prayed, "O Lord, command what You will; give what You command." St. Augustine realized he could do nothing in his own strength, and also knew that God Himself understood this most of all. This thought, however, annoyed Pelagius (d. 420 or 440), and he became Augustine's theological rival. Pelagius championed free will, teaching that people were born without a fallen nature, foolishly implying that they are capable of obedience in themselves without the need of the Spirit. But Augustine rightly felt otherwise; that we can do nothing except by the Holy Spirit. He perceived, moreover, that God does not ask us to do what we cannot do. God supplies the grace. As Charles Wesley's (1707–1788) hymn put it, "All my help from Thee I bring."

In the same way, then, God graciously stoops to our lowly level and not only tells us what we should do but often shows why we should do it. His commands are *always* for our own good. I do not say that God tells us *every time* why we should do this or that—or that He explicitly appeals to our own interests every time He issues a command. But if you and I get to know the God of the Bible and His *ways*, we will perceive that *all* His commands are pure and just. They are "more precious than gold, than much pure gold; they are sweeter than honey, than honey from the comb. By them is your servant warned; in keeping them there is *great reward*" (Psalm 19:10–11, emphasis added). Yes. *Great reward* is promised to those who affirm God's Word.

Consider tithing, for example, a subject to which I shall return later in this book. What Abraham did on his own—to give tithes without any Law in force (see Genesis 14:20)—Moses made legal under the Law of Moses later on (see Leviticus 27:30). In other words, Abraham did not have to do this—but did; Israel after 1300 BC had to tithe—but many did not. So what did God do? He motivated them, finding their entry point—self-interest. "Bring the whole tithe into the storehouse. . . . Test me in this . . . and see if I will not throw open the floodgates of heaven and pour out *so much blessing* that you will not have room enough for it" (Malachi 3:10, emphasis added). If that word of encouragement had not been added by the prophet Malachi in this passage, I dare say that countless hundreds of thousands—no doubt millions—would *never* have been motivated to tithe their income over the centuries. Malachi's word has probably been the single greatest encouragement for Christians to tithe of any passage in the Bible. And yet it came when the Mosaic Law was still in force—when it was the *duty* of the people of God to tithe. God did not have to speak to their self-interest. But He did.

This is one of the tender ways of God. Does this surprise you? And yet—without meaning to be unfair—I have come across Christians who feel it is *beneath* them to be motivated according to their self-interest. It is as though some feel they never need this, that they would be motivated to please God, glorify God, obey God and worship Him *without any encouragement* except for their very love for God alone. As if people were that holy in themselves! People like this utterly lack objectivity about themselves and seem not to know how self-righteous they are when they disdain being motivated out of self-interest. Consider this hymn:

> My God, I love Thee; not because
> I hope for heaven thereby,

Nor yet because who love Thee not
Are lost eternally.

Thou, O my Jesus, Thou didst me
Upon the Cross embrace;
For me didst bear the nails and spear,
And manifold disgrace,

And griefs and torments numberless,
And sweat of agony;
Even death itself; and all for one
Who was Thine enemy.

Then why, most loving Jesus Christ,
Should I not love Thee well
Not for the sake of winning heaven;
Or of escaping hell;

Not with the hope of gaining aught,
Not seeking a reward;
But as Thyself has loved me,
O ever-loving Lord?

Even so I love Thee, and will love,
And in Thy praise will sing,
Solely because Thou art my God,
And my eternal King.

However seemingly majestic these words may be—attributed to St. Francis Xavier (1506–1552)—they will appeal no doubt to some sincere Christians. But I am afraid that these lines, convincing and noble though they may appear to be, could appeal to our self-righteous instincts. For no biblical writer claimed to love God without respect to any reward. The Bible teaches the very opposite.

The truth is, nobody is that spiritual, that is, that he or she does not need motivation to do the right thing. As John the

Baptist said, "A man can receive only what is given him from heaven" (John 3:27). Paul said, "Who makes you different from anyone else? What do you have that you did not receive? And if you did receive it, why do you boast as though you did not?" (1 Corinthians 4:7). We all are what we are by the sheer grace of God. If, then, you tell me that you do not need motivation along the lines of your self-interest, you are saying that you have been given grace already not given to me—making you one better! The truth is, we are all from the same "lump of clay" (Romans 9:21) and can do no good except by God's mercy. Whether it be conversion or coming into one's inheritance, it does not "depend on man's desire or effort, but on God's mercy" (Romans 9:16).

Climbing Down

In 1970 I underwent a major life decision. I began to wonder if I had been foolish in not finishing Trevecca Nazarene University (having hastily left there in 1956) and then going to a theological seminary as many do who want to be very useful in the ministry. First, I did not want to admit that I had made a mistake by leaving Trevecca; and second, I used as an excuse that the great Spurgeon did not attend a university or seminary—so why should I? That is, until someone had the cheek to say to me, "But, R. T—you're no Spurgeon." Oh dear. That led to an ever-increasing uncomfortable feeling way down deep in my soul that perhaps I should swallow my pride.

And, yet, I do recall how I would attend Southern Baptist Conventions and Pastors' Conferences, having to listen to many mediocre speakers and knowing I would never be invited because, unlike them, I had not been to seminary. I hated to admit I was so wrong and filled with self-pity. It would mean that I go back to Trevecca on bended knee, and then apply for seminary. Yes, I was being motivated to pursue further formal education in order to have a wider ministry.

But I needed to be absolutely sure. I had reckoned for years that I was fairly well versed in Scripture, that I already knew the Gospel, and that I did not expect to learn anything from a university or seminary that I truly needed in order to be effective. Not only that, I would be at least 40 years old by the time this educational process was over. But I asked myself: Which is better—to have, say, 30 years left for ministry now at my age of 35, or, when I am 40, to have 25 years left? I knew in my heart of hearts that I should climb down, go to a university and then seminary (and beyond); I would be so glad I had done all this when I was actually 40. But I still needed to know for sure.

What I then did on that afternoon in June 1970 at a Southern Baptist Convention being held in Denver, Colorado, is not something I widely recommend, and I share this guardedly with fear and trembling and some blushing. But I will come clean and admit that I asked God would He—please this one time—speak to me in His Word by letting me turn to a verse that would clearly confirm whether or not I should get more education and then at the age of 40 have my formal education behind me? As my heart began to beat harder and harder I had a strange feeling I was going to get a definite answer. I opened my little New Testament and my eyes fell directly on these words: "Moses was learned in all the wisdom of the Egyptians, and was mighty in words and deeds. And when he was full forty years old, it came into his heart to visit his brethren the children of Israel" (Acts 7:22–23 KJV). God did not have to do that for me. But He did.

That was one of the clearest words I ever received. I turned immediately to Louise and said, "We are going to resign our church [Lauderdale Manors Baptist Church in Fort Lauderdale, Florida] and get my education." I never looked back. I was actually 41 by the time I completed all I ended up doing—completing Trevecca, Southern Baptist Theological Seminary and Oxford, but I never once doubted that God stooped to my weakness that day in Denver and motivated me to do what I absolutely needed to do. It would be fifteen years after my decision before I got to address the Southern Baptist Pastor's Conference—in Dallas in 1985. But it happened. Dr. O. S. Hawkins arranged for me to speak to thirty thousand pastors, being the speaker just before the late Dr. W. A. Criswell spoke. It was worth waiting for.

"To thine own self be true," said Shakespeare. I had for years denied to myself my truest sense of regret for leaving Trevecca and avoiding the need for further schooling. I was not being truly spiritual to say that I did not need to pursue further academic training and promise that I would simply double up on praying, fasting, reading my Bible and gaining more preaching experience (I was in the pulpit and happily settled in my Fort Lauderdale church). I began to see that mature spirituality was being ruthlessly objective and true to oneself, and quit trying to appear pious by avoiding further training. The truth is, I was not that spiritual!

Why Be a Christian?

So when people say to me, "If there were no heaven or no hell I would still be a Christian" (and I *do* know what they mean by that), I think of the apostle Paul who admitted the opposite! He actually said, "If only for this life we have hope in Christ, we are to be pitied more than all men" (1 Corinthians 15:19). "Don't talk to me about Christianity if there is no heaven to look forward to," he was saying. Ask Paul if he would still be a Christian when he was "hungry and thirsty . . . in rags . . . brutally treated . . . homeless" and there was no heaven to come. Ask him what it was like to be "the scum of the earth, the refuse of the world" (1 Corinthians 4:11–13). Ask him if he would be a Christian if there were no heaven to gain when he was receiving the 39 stripes, beaten with rods, going without sleep, cold and naked (see 2 Corinthians 11:24–27). He would say, "You must be joking."

But because Christ *has risen from the dead* we know that our faith is valid and heaven is coming!

The primary reason God sent His Son to die on a cross for our sins was so that we might believe—and have eternal life and not perish—that is, not go to hell. The Bible in a nutshell is this: "For God so loved the world that he gave his one and only Son, that whoever believes in him shall not perish but have eternal life" (John 3:16).

One of my first converts at Westminster Chapel—Jay Michael, a Jewish international businessman from Los Angeles—was absolutely transformed by the Gospel. But he said to me after a couple of years, "I was a happy man until I became a Christian." He took a stand for the Gospel and never looked back. But the first sermon he heard me preach—it led to his immediate conversion—was on heaven. That gripped him.

Abuse of Motivation

It has become a sad day for Christianity when so many TV evangelists appeal to people's greed to motivate them to give financially. "God will bless you if you give to my ministry," some are saying. What is more, there is truth to this. They are motivating people to do what may be worthwhile, yes. But there is also such a thing as an ambition that has its origin from below (see James 315). It is wicked. God never appeals to our *sinful* instincts to move us to obedience. God does motivate us to give with the view of being blessed—no doubt about that; but this teaching can be abused and perverted. And I fear this is done too often!

If I went by what some TV ministers preach (and I often try to listen to them through the eyes and ears of non-Christians), I honestly and truly get the impression that—if I went by what they teach—the reason Jesus died on the cross was for our financial blessing. It must make the angels cringe. It is all about money, these preachers seem to be saying. Some TV ministers I know apparently *cannot* get through a single telecast without bringing in their hearers' financial concerns. They do this in order to get financial support for their ministries. What is more, it works! This is how they stay on the air (and some of them live in extraordinary luxury). A recent poll has revealed that, whereas thirty years ago the common denominator of charismatic/Pentecostal Christians was the gifts of the Holy Spirit, today it is prosperity teaching.

But our heavenly Father does tap in to our basic God-given instincts. He uses sex to drive one to marriage, ambition to motivate one to service—and success and fear to drive a person to faith.

God has done this from the beginning.

Going for the Gold

The LORD had said to Abram, "Leave your country, your people and your father's household and go to the land I will show you. I will make you into a great nation and I will bless you; I will make your name great, and you will be a blessing. I will bless those who bless you, and whoever curses you I will curse; and all peoples on earth will be blessed through you."

Genesis 12:1–3

By faith Moses, when he had grown up, refused to be known as the son of Pharaoh's daughter. He chose to be mistreated along with the people of God rather than to enjoy the pleasures of sin for a short time. He regarded disgrace for the sake of Christ as of greater value than the treasures of Egypt, because he was looking ahead to his reward.

Hebrews 11:24–26

Hard days are the best because that's how champions are made. If you can push through the hard things, you can push through anything.

Gabby Douglas,
sixteen-year-old gold medalist,
London Olympics 2012

Luck has nothing to with it, because I have spent many, many hours, countless hours, on the court working for my one moment in time, not knowing when it would come.

Serena Williams,
winner of four Olympic gold medals
and ranked World No. 1 in women's singles tennis

Coming into the inheritance God has chosen for us does not come easily. As the children of Israel had to fight for every inch of land God allotted to them, so you and I must wage war against the world, the flesh and the devil if we are to come into the inheritance that is rightfully ours.

We have seen how Olympic champions have to train for years in order to reach their goals. Why should you and I fancy that as Spirit-filled believers we can perfunctorily bow our heads and say a little prayer, then expect God to jump in on our behalf to make things happen for us? If Paul had to beat his body and make it his "slave" lest he be rejected for the prize (see 1 Corinthians 9:27), why should you and I be any different? Indeed, Paul said that we "wrestle" not against flesh and blood but against the demonic forces that want to destroy us (Ephesians 6:12).

We are not any different—that is, if we want to receive all that we are entitled to as children of God. And yet it means going for the gold.

Why should we not go for the gold? We can *all* receive the prize—every single one of us. Having such an aspiration is the quintessence of sanctified ambition. Such an ambition is noble, pure, God-honoring and . . . achievable. It is a goal that God approves of. After all, it is doing it for Him. Nothing glorifies Him more than His children receiving Christ's "Well done"— which is a thousand times better than an Olympic gold medal.

I referred to Moses and Abraham in the previous chapter. We return to them in some detail now. They were the two greatest men in the Old Testament. They accomplished the most of any servant of God between the Fall in the Garden of Eden and the coming of Jesus.

These two men also suffered the most. They were also the only two people in the Old Testament to be called friends of God.

Abraham: Father of the Faithful

Abraham was Exhibit A for Paul's doctrine of justification by faith, but also for a Christian coming into his or her inheritance. In Romans 4 Paul reveals both: justifying faith (how we are saved) and persistent faith (how we come into our inheritance). Abraham is our example, the Old Testament's prototype Christian.

In Genesis 15 we find a discouraged Abraham. He was a wealthy man but had no heirs and lamented that he had only his servant Eliezer to leave his wealth to. He was also an old man, and his wife, Sarah, was seemingly too old to have a baby. God simply told Abraham to "count the stars." Abraham started counting, but there were too many stars to count. God said to him, "So shall your offspring be" (Genesis 15:5). Abraham might have said, "Do You expect me to believe that?" He could have said, "Don't joke with me; don't tease me like that." But guess what: Abraham believed it! God was pleased. He actually believed this promise—which seemed completely absurd—that he would be a father in his old age. His faith, believing God—nothing else—was counted as "righteousness" in God's sight (Genesis 15:6). Righteousness was then and there *imputed* to Abraham, that is, put to Abraham's credit *as though he was* truly righteous. That does not mean he was righteous in himself; it means that *God* considered him righteous by Abraham's faith alone.

Abraham became known as the father of the faithful (see Romans 4:12). The time was approximately 1700 BC. The "gospel in advance" was preached to Abraham (see Galatians 3:8). We, too, will be counted righteous if we believe the Gospel, namely, that Jesus Christ died for our sins and was raised from the dead. This is the message of the New Testament: Rely on the blood of Jesus (plus nothing) and your faith will be counted as righteousness. Some reply: "Nonsense. Do you expect me to believe that?" But others reply: "I do believe this, that Jesus died for me and was raised from the dead." When we believe this Gospel, righteousness is instantly imputed to us as it was to Abraham. God sees us as righteous from then on. We may not feel righteous. People may see us and say, "You don't look righteous to me." But God says, "You are righteous in My sight." And that is what matters—God's opinion. Nothing more. His verdict is good enough for me. If *He* declares me righteous because I believe His Son died for me and rose from the dead, I am going to *enjoy* that sweet word—and live by it!

There now follows an intriguing study of how this same Abraham got started. He had been a moon worshiper. He had no religious pedigree, no preparation for grace and no aspiration to be seen as righteous. But one day the true God tapped Abraham on the shoulder, telling him to leave country and family and start walking. Where was he to go? Abraham had no idea. But he started, not knowing where he was going (see Hebrews 11:8).

What motivated Abraham to leave home and head for a land that God would later show him? You may be surprised. God found an entry point in Abraham.

God promised that He would make the *name* of Abraham "great." Indeed, *I will make your name great.* Why did God tell Abraham that? Was this necessary? Did this promise to Abraham—that he would have a great name—have any bearing on whether or not he would obey? Of course it did. Keep in mind, too, that it was no small ordeal for Abraham to leave home. It was a huge upheaval for Abraham—to leave not only his country but also his family and go to a "land" that would presumably be identified down the road. Abraham's accepting God's call was not disconnected from the promise that his name would be made "great." God also told him that he would be made into a "great nation" (which implies heirs), that he would indeed be *blessed.* Not only that: Those who blessed Abraham would be blessed and those who cursed him would be cursed. And if that were not enough to motivate him, God added that "all peoples of the earth" would be blessed through him. Abraham believed God and started a journey that led to blessing he could not have dreamed of.

How did Abraham know he was not deceived? He had no evidence, only God's word to him. Furthermore, there were no Bibles in those days. How did it happen? Who knows? God could have appeared to Abraham via an extraordinary vision. Perhaps He did. Perhaps God sent a glorious angel with heavenly radiance that was so overwhelming that Abraham knew he was not being deceived. Or is it possible that God spoke to Abraham in an audible voice that was utterly undeniable? Perhaps. All the above and other ways it could have happened are possible. But keep in mind something absolutely essential to this discussion: God would never speak to Abraham in a manner that would eliminate the need for *faith*.

There are two worldviews of faith: (1) the secular or humanistic view—seeing is believing—and (2) the biblical view—believing without seeing. So whether it was a vision, an angel or an audible voice that secured the positive response in Abraham, he would only proceed by *faith*. Faith is the assurance of things hoped for but without the evidence (see Hebrews 11:1). And Hebrews tells us that what Abraham did was carried out by faith—believing God.

This explains why God stooped to Abraham's point of interest to motivate him. If it was only the sovereign work of the Spirit (without any further motivation) that secured Abraham's obedience, why did God *bother* to motivate him? Why get his attention with the promise of greatness and being a blessing to the world if his obedience would follow without motivation? Why tell Abraham that all who bless him will be blessed and all who curse him will be cursed?

You may say that Abraham's call was surely the effectual calling by the Holy Spirit. Agreed. You may regard Abraham's calling as nothing but the sovereign work of the Holy Spirit. Granted. But the Holy Spirit applies the word we hear. And that word connected with Abraham's mind and heart. God knows how to secure the response He wants in us. He has a thousand ways to do it. But it will always be a case of God—who knows each of us backward and forward—knowing how to get our attention. And so God found an entry point in Abraham that was so appealing to him that Abraham started walking.

That said, it is nonetheless true that whatever it was that got Abraham to leave home, it was still a case of believing without seeing. The effectual calling still required him—and all of us—to have faith.

Believing God's word is what *justified* Abraham. But *persisting* in that faith is what led to Abraham coming into his inheritance. As with all of us, our inheritance may consist in more than one thing. There is the internal—believing God—and the external—things we eventually get to see. Now, here is the amazing thing with Abraham. He had been promised the land of Canaan as an inheritance. But according to Stephen he did not even get "a foot of ground" (Acts 7:5). Whatever is going on? As John Calvin noted, it must have occurred to Abraham that he had been deceived. He must have felt betrayed. But he did what we all are called to do—sooner or later: break the betrayal barrier.

I reckon most Christians give up too soon when they feel that God lets them down. As a consequence of their not persisting in faith, such people never know what "might have been," that is, what would have happened had they persisted and not given up. Abraham persisted. Although he did not get a "foot of ground" in Canaan, he got to see God work powerfully in a manner that was far greater than the land of *Canaan*. How about the *whole world*? He with his offspring would be "heir of the world" (Romans 4:13)!

Dr. Michael Eaton says it is a biblical principle that when God appears not to keep His word He gives a substitute instead—but which is far better than what was originally promised. Those described in Hebrews 11, for example, did not receive what was promised (see Hebrews 11:39), but they accomplished far more than they ever dreamed—by persisting in faith. The world was not worthy of them (see Hebrews 11:38). But they turned the world upside down in their generation and became legends.

As for Abraham, he not only broke the betrayal barrier by persisting in faith without getting "a foot of ground" in Canaan but was required by God to sacrifice Isaac. "Take your son, your only son, Isaac, whom you love . . . [and] sacrifice him" (Genesis 22:2). Talk about feeling betrayed! But he broke the betrayal barrier and experienced something that one can only describe as absolutely extraordinary: to experience God Himself *swearing an oath*. You could infer that Abraham's internal inheritance was doubled: (1) by great faith he believed Sarah would conceive and give birth to Isaac (see Romans 4:19–21); and (2) he experienced God swearing an oath to him (see Genesis 22:16; Hebrews 6:13–14). As for the external inheritance of Abraham, he saw little of it—except (mainly) for the birth of Isaac. That said, the rest of his external inheritance speaks for itself: his role in the Old Testament, his place in the New Testament and the fact that you and I are a part of his family!

My point is this: Abraham's faith increased and matured into a profound motivation to please God alone. It got launched with the promise of greatness. But at some stage in his pilgrimage Abraham moved from an ambition that saw greatness and glory down the road to a consuming desire only to please and obey God. That was all that mattered to Abraham in the end. God got his attention early on, but Abraham's ambition matured to the degree he only wanted to please God. That is the way it must be with you and me, too.

Moses: Choosing the Reward

"Comparisons are onerous," said Shakespeare. But if you were forced to choose the single greatest person in the Old Testament, it would be Moses. The whole of the Old Testament is summed up in one name—*Moses*; the whole of the New Testament is summed up in one name—*Jesus*. "For the law was given through Moses; grace and truth came through Jesus Christ" (John 1:17).

But would it surprise you to discover that Moses was initially motivated by *reward*? Had you thought that, surely, motivation by getting a reward is beneath such a great and godly man? And yet the greatest figure between the Fall of humankind and the coming of Jesus—the man chosen by God to deliver Israel from Pharaoh and to give us the Law—was moved by *faith* to pursue a reward. "He regarded disgrace for the sake of Christ as of greater value than the treasures of Egypt, because he was looking ahead to his reward" (Hebrews 11:26; "recompense of the reward," KJV). This means that Moses made a calculated, pragmatic decision. He chose the shame of suffering for Christ over the riches and power of Egypt for one reason: The reward for persistent faith was better! But how could suffering for Jesus Christ be more valuable than the prestige of Egypt—with all the comfort and glory that goes with being a part of the Royal Family? Or how could bearing the "disgrace" for the sake of Christ be more precious than the luxury and wealth of Egypt?

Answer: The *reward* that would be coming. Moses was given to see by the Holy Spirit what he would inherit from God down the road if he identified with the Israelites. He discerned that God's approval was worth much, much more than Egyptian wealth and security—more than anything he could receive by remaining known as the grandson of Pharaoh.

But however could this be done for the "sake of Christ"? Moses lived in around 1300 BC, so how could he do what he did for the sake of Jesus Christ, who had not yet even come to the earth? I reply: In the same way that the Gospel was preached in advance to Abraham as when God said, "Count the stars," with reference to his seed (Genesis 15:5; Galatians 3:8ff), so also was the stigma of our Lord Jesus Christ inherent in the ministry God had designed for Moses. Not that he saw Jesus as clearly as you and I do now, but Moses nonetheless discerned there would be not a little suffering when making his major decision. Not only that, Moses' greater mission would be to unveil the Law that would be ultimately fulfilled in the Person and work of Jesus Christ on the cross. In a word, what Moses did was to embrace what would one day be the exact same kind of offense that would accompany all of us who would embrace Jesus Christ.

Moses made this decision at the age of forty (see Acts 7:22–23). He had been brought up in the palace of King Pharaoh. Moses had plenty of time to taste fine dining, ease, earthly glory and security. He had it all. Everything. But he knew he was not Egyptian and that those Israelites who had been enslaved by the king were of his flesh and blood. In a word, he was one of them. When the realization of this burned ever-increasingly in him and he could take it no longer, he decided to visit his brothers. But Moses mishandled things, getting off to a horrible start. What he thought would endear him to his brothers the Israelites—by his killing an Egyptian—totally backfired. It was evident to everyone that Moses had murdered an Egyptian citizen; he was suddenly a hunted and wanted man. Moses had not expected this and realized he had no choice but to flee the wrath of the king. He knew he would suffer, yes; but not so soon or in the way it turned out. In any case Moses escaped and was not seen for another forty years (see Exodus 2:11–15; Acts 7:22–30).

Moses' internal inheritance emerged one day when he saw a bush on fire that did not burn up. When he saw this sight and tried to figure it out he heard God speak, calling him by name: "Moses! Moses! . . . Take off your sandals, for the place where you are standing is holy ground" (Exodus 3:4–5). You could obviously argue that this manifestation was external not internal. But this was an angelic vision—a phenomenon wholly supernatural. Furthermore, the manner in which God continued to speak—informing Moses that he would be the deliverer to the children of Israel—was part of his internal inheritance. And yet the plagues that would follow, though supernatural, were external.

My point is, Moses refused "by faith" to be known as the son of Pharaoh's daughter (Hebrews 11:24). It was by faith that he envisaged the reward. There is no evidence of the manifest presence of God during those early years. We are only told that he eschewed the pleasures of sin for a season and that he was "looking ahead to his reward" (Hebrews 11:25–26). It seems then that the first evidence of a reward was the burning bush experience. But after that God began to speak with Moses often. It was a wonderful reward from God for Moses to have this kind of intimacy with the Almighty. The ten plagues upon Pharaoh and Egypt culminated in the Passover Lamb and the killing of the firstborn in Egypt. Such phenomena were both supernatural and yet physical. It was part of Moses' external inheritance. Then came the miraculous crossing over the Red Sea as on dry land. The Ten Commandments and the details of the Law came in the wilderness. Moses experienced the immediate and direct presence of God when the glory of the Lord covered the Tent of Meeting. The supernatural was evident in the wilderness for the next forty years through the manna and the guidance by the pillar of fire and cloud (Exodus 40:36–38). Moses' inheritance was the most spectacular and prodigious of any figure in the Old Testament. Remember, his reward is summed up in these words: "For the Law was given through Moses; grace and truth came through Jesus Christ" (John 1:17).

But Moses also suffered—perhaps more than anybody. Beginning with his abrupt rejection by his Israelite brothers, he faced this forty years later when he went to them again. Accepted with great delight at first, he was soon upbraided because things moved so slowly. He was challenged by his fellow Israelites when Pharaoh required them to get their own straw to make the same number of bricks. He suffered constantly under Pharaoh's recalcitrance when getting the king's promise to let the people go—and then Pharaoh changing his mind. All this time he had to keep the people of Israel as content as possible. His leadership consisted in doing what had never been done before—instructing the children of Israel to sprinkle blood over the doorposts when the Death Angel would pass through the land and kill all firstborn. Only those where the blood had been sprinkled over the doors had any safety. God said, "When I see the blood, I will pass over you" (Exodus 12:13). All the supernatural deliverances were not enough to keep complainers quiet. Opposition from his own people continued on and on every time things went wrong. Rebellion to Moses' leadership came again and again in the wilderness—e.g., from Aaron, Miriam, Korah and others.

And yet Moses was the greatest leader the world has ever known. He stood by his people and prayed for them when God offered to destroy them and start with a new nation (see Numbers 14:11–20). But there is a principle that is to be seen with the people of God: The greater the anointing, the greater the suffering. Winston Churchill said, "The price of greatness is responsibility." But it is also true that when it comes to our inheritance in the Kingdom of God—and that suffering is accepted with dignity and without grumbling—the greater the suffering, the greater the anointing. A call to greatness is a call to pain.

As I said in the preface, this book began to be written during and immediately following the time of the 2012 London Olympics. It was so hard to hold back the tears when watching the Gabby Douglases and the Serena Williamses of this world receiving their gold medals and hearing the national anthems playing. What a feeling it must be—what we all would feel—if we actually got into their skins during that brief poignant moment! I cannot imagine a greater feeling of more extreme joy and sense of gratitude.

And yet I can; it would be at the moment, and it will be coming, when at the Judgment Seat of Christ Jesus Himself looks straight at us—right into our eyes—and says, "Well done." We will experience an incalculable euphoria that will last not merely for a few seconds but will stay with us throughout eternity. His "Well done" will be worth all the effort, all the struggle, the hurt, lies, hate, the tears, misunderstanding, suffering, loneliness, pain and rejection we will have undergone on this earth for the sake of Christ. It will be worth it all. And it will come to us—all because we made the decision to follow Jesus and go for the gold.

The Original Ambition

How you have fallen from heaven, O morning star, son of the dawn! You have been cast down to the earth, you who once laid low the nations! You said in your heart, "I will ascend to heaven; I will raise my throne above the stars of God; I will sit enthroned on the mount of assembly, on the utmost heights of the sacred mountain. I will ascend above the tops of the clouds; I will make myself like the Most High." But you are brought down to the grave, to the depths of the pit.

Isaiah 14:12–15

Now the serpent was more crafty than any of the wild animals the LORD God had made. [The serpent said to the woman,] "God knows that when you eat of [the Tree of the Knowledge of Good and Evil], your eyes will be opened, and you will be like God, knowing good and evil." When the woman saw that the fruit of the tree was good for food and pleasant to the eye, and also desirable for gaining wisdom, she took some and ate it. She also gave some to her husband, who was with her, and he ate it. Then the eyes of both of them were opened, and they realized they were naked; so they sewed fig leaves together and made coverings for themselves.

Genesis 3:1–7

What made Adam and Eve sin? Ambition came into it, and ambition taking a particular form and the form was this. It was a desire for a short road to divine knowledge. . . . The ultimate trouble with most false doctrines and especially most doctrines of sanctification is that they are trying to arrive at something by means of a shortcut and you see that that was the original cause of man's downfall.

D. Martyn Lloyd-Jones (1899–1981)

One of Satan's most powerful ways of defeating us is to get us to believe a lie. And the biggest lie is that there are no consequences to our own doing. Satan will give you whatever you ask for if it will lead you where he ultimately wants you.

Charles Stanley (b. 1932)

We are looking at the good, the bad and the ugly when it comes to ambition and motivation. Ambition is not a vice or virtue in itself; it depends upon the motivation that lies behind the goal—and what that goal is.

The first ambition to be seen in the universe that God made is not to be found either in men or women, but in the heart of Satan before God created us. First called "morning star, son of

70

the dawn" (Isaiah 14:12; "Lucifer, son of the Morning," KJV), Satan was driven by an evil ambition—to be like God and be even greater than God.

Satan, though created by God, is a fallen angel. He was arguably the highest, most brilliant and greatest of God's creatures before God made humankind. But Satan was not created fallen; that fallen state was a permanent and irrevocable position he inherited owing to his choice. All things were created by Jesus Christ, "things in heaven and on earth, visible and invisible, whether thrones or powers or rulers or authorities; all things were created by him and for him" (Colossians 1:16). "Through him all things were made; without him nothing was made that has been made" (John 1:3).

Satan led a rebellion in heaven. He attempted to recruit every angel in heaven to join him in revolting against the Most High God. It is possible that one third of the angels joined Satan, certainly if Revelation 12:4 is pointing to that event. These angels did not keep their original positions of authority. They abandoned their own home. God has kept them ever since "in darkness, bound with everlasting chains for judgment on the great day" (Jude 6). These demonic powers were first deceived by Satan and then taken captive by God. God did not spare the angels when they sinned but "sent them to hell [Gr. *Tartarus*], putting them into gloomy dungeons to be held for judgment" (2 Peter 2:4). The Final Judgment—the Judgment Seat of Christ—will comprise judging not only the saved and lost but also Satan and all who were a part of his conspiracy.

It was *ambition*—vain ambition—that motivated Satan to conspire against God. He somehow imagined he could rival God and be greater than God. Satan wanted the ultimate authority and power in the heaven of heavens. That became his driving motivation at some point after he was created and (presumably) before the creation of the Garden of Eden.

Jesus' Temptations

Satan still claims to have this power. Appealing to Jesus' human nature during the forty days He was tempted by the devil, Satan took him "to a very high mountain and showed him all the kingdoms of the world and their splendor." Then Satan said to Jesus, "All this I will give you . . . if you will bow down and worship me" (Matthew 4:8). That was a lie. Satan did not have that power or authority at all to deliver this. Never forget: Satan is a liar and is the father of lies (see John 8:44).

Whether Jesus was tempted truly to take seriously the devil's absurd claim, I tend to doubt. But perhaps He was. For this temptation was absolutely real. It was intended to appeal directly to Jesus' ego, sense of personal esteem and ambition. Satan was tempting Jesus with the same desires that motivated him when rebelling against God. We may assume that Satan thought he might bring Jesus down through pride, the same motivation that governed him. Satan succeeded with Adam and Eve. But the "last Adam" said, "Away from me, Satan! For it is written: 'Worship the Lord your God, and serve him only'" (Matthew 4:10).

Jesus was actually "led by the Spirit into the desert to be tempted by the devil" (Matthew 4:1). This fact of the Holy Spirit's guidance is sufficient to show that the temptations of Jesus were very real. The following forty days were part of Jesus' preparation to become our Great High Priest. Preparation for *Jesus*? Surely not! Was He not the eternal Son of God? Yes. But incredible though it may seem, "he learned obedience from what he suffered" (Hebrews 5:8). Indeed, "Because he himself suffered when he was tempted, he is able to help those who are being tempted" (Hebrews 2:18). To put it another way, when we are tempted to vain ambition, Jesus understands. He does not moralize us but is able to sympathize since He faced the same thing.

God does not tempt us. "When tempted, no one should say, 'God is tempting me.' For God cannot be tempted by evil, nor does he tempt anyone" (James 1:13). But God may set us up for it! He did this with Abraham when He "tested" him (Genesis 22:1). That is precisely what lay behind Jesus' temptation in the wilderness; it was God's setup.

Jesus was "tempted in every way, just as we are—yet was *without sin*" (Hebrews 4:15). The phrase *without sin* refers to the fact that Jesus never—ever—succumbed to the devil's temptation. But this phrase also refers to the fact that Jesus had a sinless nature. This shows that one does not have to be *sinful* to be tempted. Adam was tempted before he sinned. But *our* temptation—that is, with you and me—is never disassociated from a sinful nature. We are tempted when we are drawn away by our own "evil desire" (James 1:14). But also remember that there is a difference between temptation and sin. It is *not* a sin to be tempted; it is only sin when you give in to the temptation. It is not a sin to be ambitious. Ambition becomes sinful when it is not subservient to a love for the honor of God. To put it another way, you and I will be tempted but—unlike Jesus—we also have a sinful nature. Jesus was "without sin." He came in the "likeness" of sinful flesh (Romans 8:3), but He did not have a sinful nature.

In this way Jesus could be compared to Adam prior to the Fall in the Garden of Eden. Adam before the Fall and Jesus had in common a sinless nature. Adam was created "able to sin"—*posse peccare*, as St. Augustine put it. Jesus was the "second man" or "last Adam" (see 1 Corinthians 15:45–47). Jesus did what Adam did not do, namely, to obey the will of God. Jesus, therefore, succeeded where Adam failed. Jesus lived without ever sinning, always pleasing the Father.

To determine fully how strong Jesus' sense of ambition was when He was tempted in the wilderness—or afterward—would be to delve into unprofitable speculation. And yet we may safely assume Jesus was weakened in His body from not eating for forty days. The temptation to pride and vain ambition was the final attempt of the devil—that is, during those forty days—to get Jesus to fall. Satan began by subtly trying to get Jesus to doubt who He was by saying, "*If* you are the Son of God," hoping Jesus would then doubt whether or not He truly was the Son of God. Then Satan attacked Jesus at His point of hunger: "Tell these stones to become bread." After that the devil, trying to destroy Jesus, told Him to jump off the pinnacle of the Temple (see Matthew 4:3–5). Then came the temptation to worship Satan in order to get the kingdoms of the world. The truth is, Jesus by inheritance was already predestined to have the kingdoms of the world! That said, it seems that Satan kept the temptation that related to pride and ambition to the last since Jesus could have been the most vulnerable by then—from hunger and weakness—to give in to a satanic lie. But Jesus never gave in. He did not do it then; He did not do it later.

Jesus, being incarnate deity, inherited a divine will and invincible motivation from the Father. Jesus, being fully God, was the guarantee that the "last Adam" would not fail. And yet His adopted father, Joseph, being Jesus' earthly role model, would have passed on to Jesus a strong sense of ambition, self-esteem, responsibility and motivation. Jesus was truly man. To deny

Jesus' full humanity is heretical; to deny His full deity is equally a heresy. Our Lord Jesus Christ was the God-man. "In the beginning was the Word, and the Word was with God, and the Word was God" (John 1:1). The Word was made "flesh" (John 1:14). Jesus was God Almighty *as though* He were not man; He was truly man *as though* He were not God. He was not 50 percent God and 50 percent man; He was 100 percent God and 100 percent man. As the perfect human being He would have had the innate drive and motivation of the healthiest ego that ever was. And yet Jesus being fully God would not fail as the first Adam had done.

Jesus' Ambition

Jesus' sole ambition and motivation was to please the Father. "I always do what pleases him," He said to the Jews (John 8:29). "The Son can do nothing by himself; he can do only what he sees his Father doing" (John 5:19). The Father said of Jesus, "With him I am well pleased" (Matthew 3:17; 17:5). Whatever drive, motivation and sense of ambition Jesus had when He walked on this earth, He channeled it in one direction in order to accomplish one thing: to fulfill the will of the Father.

Moreover, what Jesus did, you and I are required to do. And that is to lay aside *all* ambition except to please our heavenly Father. "Let this mind be in you, which was also in Christ Jesus" (Philippians 2:5 KJV). Jesus, though God, and remaining fully God, emptied Himself of the *privileges* of deity. He made Himself nothing. He made Himself of no reputation. He humbled Himself as a man. He went to the cross. He laid aside all ambition except pleasing the Father. He came to finish the work God gave Him to do (see John 4:34; 5:36). And what is more, He did it (see John 19:30)! Hallelujah, what a Savior!

Although we are told to be like Jesus and do what He did, we all fail. We have inherited Adam's fallen nature—what St. Augustine called *non posse non pecarre*—"not able not to sin." That is the state into which all men and women are born—no exceptions. Although through regeneration—being born again—we are *posse non pecarre*—"able not to sin," that does not mean we never sin. It means we are given the Holy Spirit to help us to resist temptation and sin, and seek to please God. But none of us is perfect. Jesus knew we would need the Lord's Prayer. He inserted the petition "forgive us our debts [or trespasses], as we forgive our debtors" (Matthew 6:12 KJV; see also Luke 11:4) because He knew we would need it. Indeed, if we "claim to be without sin" we are deceived and "the truth is not in us" (1 John 1:8). One day, however, we will be glorified (see Romans 8:30) when we will be *non posse pecarre*—"not able to sin." What is more, the only aspiration and motivation we will have in heaven is to glorify God. To love Him, as Robert Murray M'Cheyne put it, "with unsinning heart."

It was ambition, then, that lay behind Satan's motivation to revolt in heaven. It was also ambition that led to our parents' sin in the Garden of Eden. Dr. Martyn Lloyd-Jones called it wanting a "short road to divine knowledge." The same devil who led the revolt in the heavenlies against God came in the form of the serpent in the Garden of Eden. Satan wanted humankind to repeat what he had done in the heavens and appealed to Eve's sense of ambition to lure her to revolt against the Most High God. It was Satan's subtlety, craftiness and evil ploy at work. Whereas in the heavens Satan openly challenged God, in the Garden of Eden he came in disguise and lured Eve to think she was doing the right thing. What Paul would later refer to as Satan masquerading as an angel of light (2 Corinthians 11:14).

That was exactly what the serpent was doing. The serpent accomplished what he wanted. Instead of Eve pursuing obedience *not to eat from the Tree of the Knowledge of Good and Evil,* she chose what she now believed to be a quick and instantaneous knowledge of God. Adam followed her. They saw that the tree was "good for food" and "pleasant to the eyes." Ambition, then, was at the bottom of man's downfall.

We have seen that ambition is not necessarily a bad thing. But it tends to be bad more than good when described in the Bible. When we come to understand this, we should learn to see ambition as an amber light—use caution: Slow down and be prepared to stop. Ambition can achieve wonderful things; it can accomplish the most evil things.

Dr. Lloyd-Jones reckons that most false doctrines, especially heretical doctrines of sanctification, are traced to the wish for a quick result. I know from my own background that we were taught that "entire sanctification" comes from an instantaneous second work of grace after conversion. We were told that "inbred sin"—inherited from the Fall—is taken out. The result was being "sanctified wholly." This could allegedly happen to a very young person or to old people—or anyone in between. In other words, you could be converted yesterday and sanctified wholly today. Growth, or discipline, did not come into the picture. All one needed was to "lay your all on the altar" and the "second blessing" would come. That was it. You were now sinless. Some would say we even became like Adam in the Garden of Eden before the Fall. It was an instant experience. If only!

The truth is, we all need to grow. The reality is, sin in us will remain until we get to heaven. The further truth is, our ambition needs to be checked. Daily. All the time, seeing ambition as an amber light. The heart is deceitful above everything—desperately and incurably wicked (see Jeremiah 17:9).

The devil, speaking generally, is revealed two ways in the New Testament. He comes as a roaring lion "looking for someone to devour" (1 Peter 5:8). It is hard to miss a roaring lion! But the other way is the devil's masquerading as an "angel of light" (2 Corinthians 11:14). It is easy to be unaware and ensnared when Satan shows up this way; you might initially think "this is God at work." The greatest antidote to satanic masquerading is *knowledge*. "My people are destroyed from lack of knowledge" (Hosea 4:6). The knowledge of God's Word, His ways, His work and His wisdom are principally what will help us to recognize Satan's ways. Paul could say that he was not ignorant or unaware of the devil's schemes (2 Corinthians 2:11).

The devil will work overtime to appeal to our pride, our fragile egos and sense of self-esteem. We all want—and need—significance. This is legitimate. But a feeling of the worth that is God-given will ultimately come *only* when we resist the devil and pursue God's honor and glory.

Ambition and Spiritual Gifts

God's gifts and his call are irrevocable [without repentance, KJV]. . . . Do not think of yourself more highly than you ought, but rather think of yourself with sober judgment, in accordance with the measure of faith God has given you. . . . We have different gifts, according to the grace given us.

Romans 11:29; 12:3, 6

Now about spiritual gifts, brothers, I do not want you to be ignorant. . . . All these [wisdom, knowledge, faith, healing, miraculous powers, prophecy, distinguishing between spirits, speaking in different kinds of tongues, interpretation of tongues] are the work of one and the same Spirit, and he gives them to each one, just as he determines. . . . Are all apostles? Are all prophets? Are all teachers? Do all work miracles? Do all have gifts of healing? Do all speak in tongues? Do all interpret? But eagerly desire the greater gifts.

1 Corinthians 12:1, 11, 29–31

It was [Christ] who gave some to be apostles, some to be prophets, some to be evangelists, and some to be pastors and teachers, to prepare God's people for works of service, so that the body of Christ may be built up.

Ephesians 4:11–12

Don't bother to give God instructions; just report for duty.

Corrie ten Boom (1892–1983)

In the summer of 1974 my family and I traveled across Europe, including Haarlem, the Netherlands. We visited the Beje, the famous home and watch shop with its "Hiding Place" where Corrie ten Boom's family courageously hid Jews from the Nazis in World War II. While in Haarlem I was privileged to visit Corrie ten Boom at her home. During that hour with her I asked, "Is it true that you believe in the gifts of the Holy Spirit?" Her reply: "Yes. First Corinthians twelve and fourteen. But don't forget First Corinthians thirteen."

Back in 1956, I had come across the idea that the gifts of the Spirit "ceased" early on in Church history, namely, when the canon of Scripture was compete. The people who hold to this perspective are usually called "cessationists." My own experience, referred to earlier, when the glory of the Lord filled the car on my way from Palmer to Nashville on October 31, 1955, had changed my theology overnight. I became a Calvinist without ever hearing any teaching on it or reading any books on it. I later found some Presbyterians and Baptists who taught what had been revealed to me—except for one oddity: They were cessationists and did not believe that God operated in the supernatural nowadays. In other words, they welcomed my embracing Reformed theology but were unable to explain how I came to see this solely by the "immediate and direct witness" of the Holy Spirit, a phrase I learned from Dr. Martyn Lloyd-Jones. By *immediate and direct* he meant to show a clear distinction from the mediate and indirect, that is, when the Holy Spirit *applies* the Word. In other words, when the Holy Spirit applies the Word it is mediated; it is indirect. But when the Holy Spirit comes to a person immediately and directly—as if apart from the Word—one experiences the Holy Spirit's own very Presence. This concept was not simply important to him; it was essential to his understanding of the Holy Spirit. I remember how one Presbyterian minister rejected my experience of the Holy Spirit—when I was driving in my car—but had to admit that the flesh or the devil could not have taught me Reformed theology without any prior exposure to it.

I did not have a good introduction to the gifts of the Holy Spirit in any case. I say this for two reasons. First, my old denomination not only did *not* emphasize them but was prejudiced in particular against the gift of speaking in tongues. The Church of the Nazarene was initially called the Pentecostal Church of the Nazarene. But they were followers of John Wesley rather than accepting the outpouring of the Spirit on Azusa Street in Los Angeles in 1906 (which focused largely on tongues). As I said in the previous chapter, my old denomination emphasized two works of grace—calling the second work the "baptism with the Holy Spirit" (or entire sanctification). But they taught—and emphasized—that the baptism with the Spirit did *not* include speaking in tongues (but rather the removal of indwelling sin).

Both Nazarenes and Pentecostals had an exponential growth in the early twentieth century, with the latter becoming known for speaking in tongues. The Nazarenes voted to drop the name

"Pentecostal" as they certainly did *not* want people thinking they spoke in tongues.

In February 1956—about four months after the experience of October 31, 1955, I was given yet another experience. This time I was driving from Kentucky into Tennessee. As I was crossing the border, I felt a stirring in my innermost being. It was deep in my heart—almost as though it was in my stomach, like a well or geyser that wanted to spring up. The only way to let it spew out was to give in to it—which I did—by letting my tongue express unintelligible sounds. I would call it utter gibberish. It lasted only a couple of seconds or more. People were in the car. They must have heard me. I was embarrassed so I stopped it. But I knew I had spoken in tongues for the first time in my life. I was not seeking it, wanting it or expecting it. It just happened. No one said a word; neither did I share this with anyone for a long time. I eventually told Dr. Lloyd-Jones after I became the minister of Westminster Chapel. He regarded this experience as genuine.

The purpose of this chapter is to demonstrate not only that our ambition should be channeled in one direction—to glorify God—but that we should prove we mean this by earnestly coveting the greater gifts of the Holy Spirit—as Paul said we should do (see 1 Corinthians 12:31). It seems to me that we cannot honestly claim to want *all* there is of God if we block off openness to the Holy Spirit generally and His gifts particularly.

The Silent Divorce

I shall now repeat what I have stated many times, that there is a silent divorce in the Church, speaking generally, between the Word and the Spirit. When there is a divorce sometimes the children stay with the mother, sometimes they stay with the father.

In this divorce between the Word and the Spirit, you have those who are on the "Word" side and some on the "Spirit" side. Those on the Word side emphasize earnestly contending for the faith once delivered unto the saints—upholding the Gospel, expository preaching, a return to the doctrines of the Reformation, the "fruits" of the Spirit and sound theology. What is wrong with that emphasis? Nothing. It is exactly right.

Take those on the Spirit side; the emphasis is to get back to the book of Acts. In the earliest Church there were supernatural signs, wonders and miracles, the gifts of the Spirit were in operation, such power manifested in a prayer meeting that the place was shaken, if you got into Peter's shadow you were healed, lie to the Holy Spirit and you were struck dead. What is needed today is this kind of power. What is wrong with this emphasis? Nothing. It is exactly right.

The problem is, although there are exceptions for which I thank God, it seems that it is usually one or the other! We need *both*. I believe that the simultaneous combination will result in spontaneous combustion and the result will be the restoration of the honor of God's name.

I believe that not only the *fruits* of the Spirit are desperately needed today but also the *gifts* of the Spirit, that both are available to the Church—and always have been. There is not a shred— or even a hint—of biblical evidence that either miracles or the immediate and direct witness of the Spirit would by God's design, purpose and intent become unavailable to the Church.

The Meaning of the Spiritual Gifts

The gifts of the Spirit may ebb and flow in a person. We do not "own" the gifts in such a way that we can "switch them on."

They are gifts of the *Holy Spirit*—not ours. He owns them. You might say they are on loan to us. And yet certain gifts sometimes reside indefinitely in an individual. Many people have felt that Dr. Lloyd-Jones had the gift of wisdom. King Saul was given the gift of prophecy (see 1 Samuel 10:9–13). There is a general principle in Scripture that what God gives you cannot lose. This is why the gifts are not tied to one's repentance; they are irrevocable (see Romans 11:29).

Whereas Paul applies this principle to Israel in Romans 11:29, it is a truth that pervades generally with God's dealings with us. The sovereignty of God is the sole explanation. In the same way that we are not chosen according to our works (see 2 Timothy 1:9)—nor are we kept saved by works (see Ephesians 2:8–9)—so, too, God sovereignly bestows certain gifts on His people. And yet the people who have them cannot always make them function as they might wish. But King Saul—after he was rejected by God—was, amazingly, enabled to prophesy on his way to kill young David (see 1 Samuel 19:23–24). This demonstrates that the gifts may be present without our repentance. Whereas some people may seem to have certain gifts all the time, others do not—but only on occasion.

I question whether anyone has a particular gift at work *all* the time—but only when it is needed. God knows what we need at a given time. If any of us had some of these gifts *all the time* it would be hard not to become proud and we would probably take ourselves too seriously. We may also imagine ourselves to be spiritual when in fact the gifts are no sign of one's spirituality. This is why the fruits of the Spirit are more important and must accompany the gifts—to keep us humble. The gifts in any case are primarily given for the edification of the Body of Christ—not for the people who experience them (see 1 Corinthians 12:7, 12–26).

Wisdom

It is no accident that the gift of wisdom is put first in order (see 1 Corinthians 12:8–10). I sometimes think, however, that it is the last gift some seem to want—and the very gift we all need most! Wisdom is having the presence of the mind of the Holy Spirit. It is to have *understanding*. To have it is to envisage clearly the next step forward regarding what you should say or do. It is doing or saying exactly what you will be glad you did. It is speaking in a manner that will leave you with no regrets. Having wisdom was Solomon's first request immediately after he became king of Israel—a desire that greatly pleased the Lord (see 1 Kings 3:5–10). Wisdom is "more precious than rubies, and nothing you desire can compare with her" (Proverbs 8:11). Whereas it is listed as a "gift," never forget that we are admonished to seek it. "Wisdom is supreme; therefore get wisdom. Though it cost you all you have, get understanding" (Proverbs 4:7). As this gift is put before all the others, and since Paul said for us to desire earnestly the "greater gifts," surely wisdom— "the message of wisdom" ("word of wisdom," KJV) is what we should be most ambitious for.

Knowledge

Referred to as "message of knowledge" or "word of knowledge" (KJV), this could apply to interpreting Scripture faithfully and soundly. It is a gift I eagerly desire. But it also may refer to special information that is beyond ordinary knowledge. God will, of course, use the knowledge we have—as knowing our Bibles backward and forward—but Paul is here also referring to a special insight that comes by the immediate and direct witness of the Spirit. It overlaps with wisdom and a word of prophecy, which we will examine below. It is when the Holy Spirit drops a special word into your mind that you did not necessarily receive from knowing your Bible or having good theology. It is when you are given a word of encouragement—or caution—for another at a critical moment. A sweet Nigerian lady named Grace came to my wife one Sunday morning when Louise was distraught over a situation. Without having the faintest clue as to what was going on, Grace had one word for Louise: "Jealousy, Mrs. Kendall—that is the problem." It gave Louise incredible peace—just to know that God was aware of everything.

Faith

Faith may be defined as *believing God*; therefore, faith as a gift of the Spirit may seem strange, especially since we are justified by faith. But Paul in this case does not mean saving faith. Neither is this the persistent faith to which we are all called—as is demonstrated in Hebrews 11. The gift of faith is provided when you need extraordinary grace for a task that is confronting you. David was given this when he assured King Saul that he could slay Goliath—and did (see 1 Samuel 17:32–50). David was given this gift of faith years later—at the lowest ebb of his life just prior to his receiving the kingship—when he "found strength in the LORD his God" (1 Samuel 30:6). It is what lies behind the prayer of faith that heals the sick (see James 5:15). It is sometimes given when we pray for something and know that we *have received it* before it comes (see Mark 11:24), a grace that is probably not given to many every day. It is not only praying in the will of God but *knowing* you are praying in His will (see 1 John 5:14–15). It is not something you "work up"; either it is there or it is not.

Healing

A woman came up to me after I finished speaking in St. Andrews, Scotland, and said, "Would you pray for my headache?" I placed my hands on her head, prayed for her hurriedly and briefly, having no faith that I was aware of. I would have forgotten that incident had she not written to me four months later to say that she had terrible sinus headaches for five years, but on that day the pain was the worst ever. "When you prayed for me I felt nothing. But some four hours later I realized the headache was gone and no headache has ever returned." Does this mean I have the "gift of healing"? Possibly. I have seen a few people healed after praying for them. But not many. Some people are esteemed for having the gift of healing. It does not follow that everybody they pray for is healed. And yet if one has a lot of positive results in this area it seems reasonable to impute to them a gift of healing. It would seem that God has sovereignly given some people this very wonderful gift. But as Jesus healed people in different ways, one must not superimpose a rigid pattern on how the gift of healing might be used today—whether by laying hands on people, anointing with oil, through a handkerchief or by remote control. Paul did say "gifts" of healing, suggesting there is more than one kind (1 Corinthians 12:9).

Miraculous Powers

What is the difference between healing and miracles? Some would say that healing is gradual, miracles are instantaneous. This may be true. But John Paul Jackson points out that Jesus healed people instantly. He says that healing is the "removal" of something—of the cause of the illness or disease—e.g., demon, leprosy or cancer. A miracle, however, is more than that; it is regeneration by the Spirit—when, for example, God not only heals leprosy but grows hands and fingers. If so, miracles are exceedingly rare. Miracles refer to God stepping in and creating parts of the body—lengthening withered arms, healing blind eyes and deaf ears. God can do this as easily as curing a common cold. But for some reason He has chosen not to do this as often as some claim or we might wish. And yet I would personally desire eagerly such a gift! This would be a totally justified ambition. But since the gifts are "without repentance" (Romans 11:29 KJV), meaning that no amount of repenting on our part will persuade God to bestow such a gift, all we can do is to covet such a gift—and ask God if He would graciously grant it.

Prophecy

The gift of prophecy could include preaching but refers to a supernatural ability to reveal what God is saying *now* and—sometimes—what lies in the future. A prophetic word for the future—possibly as rare as a gift of performing the miraculous—is to be welcomed in the Church. Paul exhorted the Corinthians to desire this particular gift. These people had apparently become preoccupied with tongues. He said,

> Anyone who speaks in a tongue does not speak to men but to God. Indeed, no one understands him; he utters mysteries with his spirit. But everyone who prophesies speaks to men for their strengthening, encouragement and comfort.
>
> 1 Corinthians 14:2–3

The former edifies oneself; the latter edifies the Church (see 1 Corinthians 14:4). This gift of prophecy does *not* elevate one to the status of the Jeremiahs or Isaiahs of this world. Dr. Wayne Grudem makes a persuasive case that the canonical prophets of the Old Testament were succeeded by the New Testament *apostles* and not by having the same level of prophetic gift as Paul describes in 1 Corinthians.

Dr. Michael Eaton has shown that there are "levels" of prophecy. First, inspired Scripture—a kind of prophecy that does not exist today (see 2 Peter 1:21). The revelation of doctrine in Scripture is *final and complete*. If any person claims to speak with the same authority as Holy Scripture, he or she should be rejected categorically. Second, inspiration without revelation of new doctrine. One can be "inspired"—as when George Frederick Handel wrote the *Messiah*, or when one is preaching; but no new doctrinal revelation is implied. Third, prophetic preaching—speaking directly into one's life without the prophetic person always or necessarily realizing it. Fourth, prophecy in time of trouble—as when you are "given" what to say when you are delivered maliciously over to authority figures (see Matthew 10:19–20). But St. Augustine shrewdly observed that if God can do this when we are in trouble, He can do it also when we are preaching! Fifth, low-level prophecy, as when Agabus prophesied what would happen to Paul if he persisted in going to Jerusalem—a word, by the way, Paul disobeyed (see Acts 21:11–14).

The point is, there are undoubtedly *levels* of prophecy, and one should be modest in his or her claims to be speaking a word directly from God. That said, God may indeed give some of His people direct words of knowledge that greatly encourage or timely warn us. Two cautions: (1) Be very sure you do not go beyond the "proportion" of your faith—and talk too much; and (2) state only what is consistent with Scripture, what

Paul calls the "analogy of faith" (Romans 12:6). No prophetic utterance will be inconsistent with Scripture. If it is, it is to be rejected as false.

Distinguishing Between Spirits

This refers to the ability to tell the difference between the Holy Spirit and the demonic. One should want to discern the Holy Spirit most of all; too many, I fear, think only in terms of the demonic when it comes to this gift. The more we can recognize the *real*, the better able we will be to detect the *false*. The presence of the Holy Spirit can be manifested in several ways: for example, to give great joy, awe, good teaching, praise and worship; and there can even be a healing presence (see Luke 5:17). This gift to discern enables us to recognize if a person in the congregation is in the Spirit or out of order—whether in the flesh or being driven by an evil spirit. The demon-possessed person can be detected by someone with this gift. It does not follow, however, that such a gift necessarily carries with it the power to cast out the demon. This gift needs, therefore, to be combined with the gift of healing, if not also miracles. The cessationist—who does not recognize the authenticity of any of these gifts for today—is rendered especially helpless when confronted with the demonic. Are we to believe from them that the demonic ceased when the miraculous ceased? If so, why are we not equipped with adequate grace for these perilous times? But, thank God, these gifts are available today—and greatly needed.

Different Kinds of Tongues

As noted, the Greek word *glossa* means "tongue" or "language." Even words that are unintelligible to you and me may

90

still be a language. It could be a heavenly, or angelic, tongue but which nobody on earth would understand. There are confirmed cases, however, in which a person was enabled to speak in a foreign language recognizable only to the hearer who knew it. In cases like this, it is a wonderful encouragement—not to mention testimony. This not only encourages the person who recognizes his or her own language, but—more than that—demonstrates the supernatural. This was seen on the Day of Pentecost (see Acts 2:6). Does this mean that a gift of tongues is the same phenomenon as what the disciples received in Acts 2:4? Not necessarily. Speaking or praying in tongues as described in 1 Corinthians 14:2ff is apparently unknown to anyone—not even to the person who prays in this manner. This does not matter. Praying like this is implied in Romans 8:26–27. Paul here indicates that he prayed with groans that words cannot express. I personally believe this was praying in tongues: known only by God but praying in the will of God. It is at least one time you know you are praying in the will of God. This is one of its best uses—knowing you are praying in God's will, whatever His will may be.

Interpretation of Tongues

I sometimes think this is the rarest gift of all, and possibly one of the most abused—if not contrived. Since speaking in tongues publicly is prohibited by Paul unless it is interpreted (see 1 Corinthians 14:28), it is almost comical (do forgive me) to hear the "interpretations" that at times follow. The way to know for sure if an interpretation is right, of course, is to have two people write down the interpretation and see if they correspond. Interpretation, however, does not mean translation; the interpretation could be to convey the general meaning of the tongue. I have witnessed this when I thought it was genuine, but usually I have been a bit skeptical. This is possibly why many cessationists want to dismiss all the gifts out of hand. We must admit honestly that the gifts may be abused—or have a counterfeit imitation.

A Lopsided Focus

As for the gifts of the Spirit generally, the focus is so often on tongues. The gift of tongues is, however, at the end or bottom of the list. The greater gifts are surely wisdom, healing or prophecy. Dr. Michael Eaton believes that the greater gifts are those that advance the Word of God—the Gospel. These are the gifts we should be ambitious for. But—that said—I would have thought that if you are truly ambitious for the greater gifts you would be *willing* to start at the bottom! I do not say you have to speak in tongues to have the greater gifts. But surely one must be willing to do so. A bit of humility is needed. So how *much* do you want these greater gifts? Enough to start at the bottom? My friend Charles Carrin said he used to pray, "Lord, I want to be filled with the Spirit, but I don't want You to do anything spectacular and I *don't* want to speak in tongues. Now with that in mind, You may proceed." Surprise, surprise, nothing happened! Charles has also shrewdly observed that the gift of tongues is the *only* gift that challenges our pride. Who *wouldn't* want the gift of wisdom—or healing? No offense there. But tongues?

Paul says clearly, however, that in the same way that not all are called to be apostles, so not all speak with tongues (see 1 Corinthians 12:30). Many enthusiastic charismatics have sadly refused to accept that verse—running slipshod over it when it is so plain and clear—and have urged everybody to speak in tongues. This is not only biblically wrong but, in my opinion, their pushing tongues on people has needlessly discouraged a lot of sincere Christians, and has sometimes caused unnecessary division in churches. But lest you think I am being unkindly biased, I should tell you that speaking in tongues returned to me a few years ago, and I exercise that gift privately and unashamedly with great profit and edification, as in 1 Corinthians 14:2–4, all the time.

You will recall that God has chosen our inheritance for us (see Psalm 47:4). This includes both the external (what we do in life—e.g., job, talent) and internal (our relationship with God and the Holy Spirit).

We now look more closely at a major aspect of our internal inheritance, namely, the gifts and callings of the Holy Spirit. These may be divided into three parts: motivational, spiritual and vocational. Motivational gifts have two sides: the natural and the role of the Spirit. Paul focuses on these largely in Romans 12:3–8. The spiritual gifts, as we just saw, are seen largely in 1 Corinthians 12:8–10. The vocational gifts are seen in Ephesians 4:11–12 and 1 Corinthians 12:28–30.

There is a hierarchy of gifts and callings, some, therefore, having a higher profile in the Church than others. Paul mentions desiring the "greater gifts," which shows that some are greater than others. This sets the stage for envy in the Body of Christ, but also the need for objectivity about ourselves.

Ambition for the gifts of the Spirit comes into the picture the moment Paul exhorts us: "Eagerly desire the greater gifts" (1 Corinthians 12:31; "covet earnestly," KJV). This is saying that we should be ambitious for the greater gifts. He also says: "If anyone sets his heart on being an overseer [bishop, elder], he desires a noble task" (1 Timothy 3:1).

And yet if God sovereignly chose our inheritance for us, does this not take the issue out of our hands? Does this not mean that there is nothing we can do to twist God's arm to bestow upon us the greater gifts? Indeed, twice Paul implied the sovereignty of God with regard to the gifts. The Holy Spirit "gives them to each one, *just as he determines*" (1 Corinthians 12:11, emphasis added). Again, "God has arranged the parts in the body, every one of them, *just as he wanted them to be*" (1 Corinthians 12:18, emphasis added). I reply: Since Paul told us to desire earnestly the greater gifts, it must mean there is hope that our ambition toward them would be honored by God. He would not dangle these greater gifts like a carrot before a donkey if there were not hope in receiving them. God is not like that.

We should never let God's omniscience keep us from praying. God knows exactly what we have need of before we ask Him (see Matthew 6:8), but immediately tells us to ask Him (verse 9)! If I take the view, "God already knows what I need and promised to supply it, so I won't bother to pray," I am a fool. God knows the end from the beginning but, nonetheless, asks us to obey His Word (including preaching the Gospel to everybody even though He knows who will be saved). So, too, with the gifts of the Spirit. He gives them sovereignly, but at the end of the discussion encourages all of us to covet the greater gifts—to motivate us to ask for them.

Motivational Gifts

Motivational gifts are those mainly referred to in Romans 12:6–8, and they overlap in some ways with the gifts of the Spirit described in 1 Corinthians 12. It would be a mistake, therefore, if we pushed the distinctions between them too sharply. That said, it would appear that the gifts referred to in Romans 12 pertain somewhat to one's *natural* gift or propensity. Some people, for example, have a natural gift of teaching. If they were not Christians they would probably be teachers of some sort. But if they are converted and a part of the Body of Christ, that gift will be joined by the Holy Spirit. Such people, therefore, are motivated naturally already—saved or not. But if they become Christians, they are likely to use that gift for the Lord in the Church. The same is true for all these gifts. Some people are naturally encouragers; so Paul tells them to encourage. Some have servant hearts by nature; they should use this gift with the people of God. Some have the natural gift of leadership; if so, "let [them] govern diligently." If they have a natural gift of being sympathetic and showing mercy, "let [them] do it cheerfully" (Romans 12:8).

But do some have a natural gift to prophesy? It would seem so—in a sense. When Amos said he was not a prophet nor the son of a prophet but a shepherd (see Amos 7:14), the truth is that he was *called* to be a prophet. But this statement suggests that sometimes the gift of prophesying may run in families. In Amos's case, no. And yet he was called to be a prophet without any background in his family for it. That was his point. Some people, however, have natural discernment. Some have great powers of observation—seeing things most people do not see. Some people have natural insight and do have a propensity to call a spade a spade. They are able to cut through the nonsense on issues. So when a gift like this is sanctified, such people may be used of God prophetically. As we saw above, however, you must do it in proportion to your faith, never going beyond what the Spirit gives or beyond the Word. The aforementioned analogy of faith is comparing Scripture with Scripture, which helps you to know you have remained theologically sound and orthodox. In any case—this cannot be repeated too often—the Holy Spirit will never lead one to prophesy but what is theologically and biblically sound.

So should one eagerly desire the greater motivational gifts (whatever you may think they might be)? Almost certainly, since Paul says we should covet the greater spiritual gifts. You could say: Paul says *desire earnestly*—not pray for them or seek them. I reply: How could you eagerly desire something God has to offer and keep from asking for it in prayer?

Paul used the same logic when it came to those who were born slaves. He believed that, generally speaking, one should "remain in the situation God called him to," if, for example, he was born as a slave. But he also said: "If you can gain your freedom, do so" (1 Corinthians 7:21, 24). In other words, a person should not feel himself or herself locked in irrevocably to a situation if he or she would like to be out of it. This, then, is the kind of thinking that lies behind the sovereignly given gifts—whether motivational or spiritual.

That said, here is where ambition comes in. There are ambitious Christians around—not all of them led by the Holy Spirit. If, therefore, one is not led by the Holy Spirit but is nonetheless a part of the Church, it disrupts the family unity. Unsanctified ambition in the Church is a major cause of the lack of unity. Paul talked about "the unity of the Spirit [in] the bond of peace" (Ephesians 4:3). The unity of the Spirit prevails when the *ungrieved* Spirit in us dwells in great measure. The Holy Spirit can be grieved. What chiefly grieves the Spirit is bitterness, anger and unforgiveness (see Ephesians 4:31–32).

If I am blessed with the *ungrieved* Spirit, I will not be bitter but totally forgiving—*and* accept my gifting and affirm yours.

This is why Paul introduces the motivational gifts with this caution: "Do not think of yourself more highly than you ought, but rather think of yourself with sober judgment, in accordance with the measure of faith God has given you" (Romans 12:3). This means that we must accept the *limits* of our anointing and not promote ourselves to the level of our incompetence. God never promotes us to the level of our incompetence. So when your ambition is sanctified, you will humbly accept what you are and what you are not; neither will you resent the person who has been promoted to a greater gift—whether motivational or spiritual.

Ruth. Here is a most unusual woman—Ruth, a Moabitess, who found her heart's desire by choosing a country alien to her and staying with Naomi, an Israelite, rather than rejecting Naomi, who seemed to have little to live for. Ruth said to Naomi, "Where you go I will go, and where you stay I will stay. Your people will be my people and your God my God" (Ruth 1:16). There appears to be no hint of self-interest in this story; it is an account of selfless love and pure sacrifice. The eventual result was, however, that Ruth found an Israelite husband, Boaz, and, as a consequence of this marriage, became part of the Messianic line and was the great-grandmother of King David (see Ruth 4:21–22).

Esther. The book in the Bible that bears Esther's name is mostly about Mordecai—an amazing man. He lovingly brought up Esther (whom he had adopted) and carefully trained her to become the queen of Susa. He also instilled in her a love for her own people, the Jews. She took Mordecai's advice and shrewdly concealed her identity from the king for a while. But once the Jews were on the verge of extinction she bravely took Mordecai's further counsel, which could mean sudden death for her. Her ambition for the glory of God outweighed her desire for personal survival. She vowed to put everything that was dear to her on the line and said, "If I perish, I perish" (Esther 4:16). Mordecai helped Esther find her heart's desire; it transcended everything.

Deborah. A prophetess and woman of great stature, Deborah called Barak to get ready to fight the enemy of Israel. Barak was a weak man, a coward. He replied to Deborah that he would obey her prophetic command but only on the condition that she go with him. Her response to this was that if she went with him, the glory would go to a woman. Neither Barak nor Deborah demonstrated a very high level of personal ambition—except this: Deborah was careful to hear from God and keenly motivated to protect Barak's male ego, an admirable quality. She went with Barak. He won. But the glory went to a woman as she predicted (see Judges 4:6–23). The surprising thing, however, is that Barak—not Deborah—gets the glory in the great faith chapter of the New Testament (see Hebrews 11:32).

Vocational Gifts

Vocational gifts refer to one's leadership position in the Church—whether apostle, prophet, evangelist, pastor or teacher. Some call this the fivefold ministry of the Church. As the spiritual and motivational gifts can overlap, meaning we must not draw the distinction too sharply, so, too, with the motivational and vocational gifts. We saw that prophesying and teaching can be motivational gifts, referring to what a person's gifting may be at the natural level. Some people are born leaders, although there are degrees of leadership ability. The fivefold ministry applies mainly to those who are essentially leaders. But not all are apostles.

The apostle is listed first in order, such being the highest profile in the Church. Paul was an apostle. His gifting almost certainly included the other four ministries; that is, he was also a prophet, an evangelist, a pastor and a teacher. But not all teachers or evangelists are apostles. And yet all are in measure leaders. If one lives by the principle of Romans 12:3—thinking no more of himself than he should—there will be no rivalry among leaders. We cannot all be apostles. We cannot all be prophets.

Should a person today call himself an apostle? If indeed there are apostles today, as in Paul's day, is it necessary to call oneself by this lofty title? Cannot one function as an apostle without claiming the title? Yes, if he has the humility to do so! I do not mean to be unfair, but I have wondered why it would be necessary to adopt this title for oneself if *ambition* were not in the picture. If one is truly an apostle—and I accept that we might have them—why *claim* to be one? If one has this gift and function, would it not be self-authenticating? If one has seen the Lord (see 1 Corinthians 9:1) and does signs, wonders and miracles (see 2 Corinthians 12:12) and founds churches, who is to say apostles cannot exist today? But claiming the title is surely redundant if one is truly an apostle. There is no sign in northwest Arizona that says, "You are now looking at the Grand Canyon." Something that majestic and awesome does not need any further comment. That said, I wonder, too, about claiming to be a prophet! But being called an evangelist, pastor or teacher would not be so related to one's ego. Let *others* call us that if they like. We should not impute exalted positions to ourselves if we are truly motivated to seek the honor that comes from God only (see John 5:44).

If a person desires to be a bishop or elder, says Paul, he aspires to a noble task (see 1 Timothy 3:1). This tacitly gives approval to such an ambition. But, that said, one must not be consumed with this wish or it will lead to a downfall. If one has such an ambition, he should keep quiet about it and let God do the promoting—if indeed the desire was God-inspired.

One final caution regarding the gifts and callings of God being irrevocable (Romans 11:29; "without repentance," KJV), meaning that repentance does not guarantee getting a gift, neither will the lack of repentance necessarily cause God to withdraw the gift. You will recall that King Saul was given the gift of prophecy. But Saul also became yesterday's man, meaning that God rejected him (see 1 Samuel 18:12); neither could he be renewed to repentance (as in Hebrews 6:4–6). And yet Saul remained king for another twenty years. Never forget that he actually "prophesied" on his way to kill young David (1 Samuel 19:22–24).

This means that you and I could be exalted to high positions—and possibly keep them—whether or not we are pleasing to the Lord. This means you or I could have great spiritual gifts—and keep them—although we may lead private lives of disgrace.

The big issue is this: keeping ambition under check and making sure it is *God* who promotes us and that it is *God* we are seeking. As long as our chief ambition is to have the honor of God—and not people—we will stay in pretty good shape. A further guarantee that we will not take ourselves too seriously is that we have the fruit of the Holy Spirit.

The Fruit of the Spirit

But the fruit of the Spirit is love, joy, peace, patience, kindness, goodness, faithfulness, gentleness and self-control.

Galatians 5:22–23

And this is my prayer: that your love may abound more and more in knowledge and depth of insight, so that you may be able to discern what is best and may be pure and blameless until the day of Christ, filled with the fruit of righteousness that comes through Jesus Christ—to the glory and praise of God.

Philippians 1:9–11

You are not going to have self control because somebody prays for you to have self control. You already have self control. It is in you as a fruit of the Spirit, but it's a little teeny tiny little seed. And, nobody else can develop your fruit of the Spirit. Nobody can develop your peace but you. Nobody can develop your joy but you. Nobody can develop your patience but you. Nobody can develop your discipline and self control but you.

Joyce Meyer (b. 1943)

I like your Christ. I do not like your Christians. Your Christians are so unlike your Christ.

Mahatma Gandhi (1869–1948)

When Corrie ten Boom said to me, "Don't forget First Corinthians thirteen," she was stressing precisely what some well-meaning Christians too often forget: the need for *agape* love. Paul finished his treatment of the various spiritual gifts in the Church by concluding we should covet earnestly the "greater" gifts, then added: "And now I will show you the most excellent way" (1 Corinthians 12:31). This implies that *agape* love is more important than all the gifts of the Spirit. It also indicates that the fruit of the Spirit is more important than the gifts.

My favorite food is Indian and my favorite Indian restaurant is in Durban, South Africa—right on the Indian Ocean. When I get to eat there I think of Mahatma Gandhi, wondering if he also ate there since he lived in Durban for a while. It was there he studied Christianity and became fascinated with the Person of Jesus. But the more he asked questions and got to know some of the Christians there, the less interested he was in Christianity—a sad fact that I sometimes remind people of when I preach in South Africa. What a difference it could have made in Gandhi's life—and possibly for the nation of India— had he met some Christians who were so filled with the fruits of the Spirit that he wanted what they had! But sadly what they had he did not want.

My friend Arthur Blessitt reached into his wallet to pay his bill for a Coke he had just finished drinking at a Holiday Inn in Amman, Jordan. The waiter said to him, "Your bill has been paid for—by that man over there sitting at the end of the counter." Arthur naturally went to this total stranger to thank him for paying his bill. *"I want what you've got,"* the man said to Arthur. Arthur replied, "What do you mean?" The man who, as it turned out, was an Arab sheik said to Arthur, "I have been watching you. You have a shine and a smile on your face. Look at all these people, no one is smiling. I want what you've got." Arthur explained that he was a follower of Jesus Christ, that he carried a cross around the world in order to spread the Gospel. Arthur then shared the Gospel with that man, who immediately prayed to receive Christ. The sheik then took Arthur to the top floor of that hotel and introduced him to every leader of OPEC, to whom Arthur witnessed one by one for the next few hours.

Making a Choice

If you must make a choice between whether you are more ambitious for the gifts of the Spirit or the fruit of the Spirit, choose the fruit of the Spirit. And yet we should want the gifts and fruits *equally*. It sometimes seems that the "Word" people are quick to stress the fruits and the "Spirit" people—wittingly or unwittingly—give the impression of emphasizing mostly the gifts of the Spirit. The cessationists deny the possibility of the gifts of the Spirit being available for today, but certainly pursue the fruits of the Spirit. I believe we should be ambitious to have the greater gifts and all the fruits of the Spirit. The greatest ambition in this connection would be what Paul calls "the most excellent way"—*agape* love.

Ambitious for more of God. That is what this book comes down to. A. W. Tozer said we could have as much of God as we want. I used to question that statement, but no longer. I now believe we can indeed have as much of God as we want. But the *want* is not to be determined by our mere "feeling" (what we may think we want at a given moment) but by how much we *pursue* God, stay vulnerable and open to His beckoning and walk in all the light He gives us. In other words, we prove how much we want God by grabbing and taking full advantage of *any* opportunity that falls into our laps that has to do with pleasing God.

I made two major decisions at Westminster Chapel during my 25 years there. The first was to invite Arthur Blessitt to preach at Westminster Chapel for six Sunday nights in a row in the spring of 1982. His ministry changed me and it turned Westminster Chapel upside down. The second major decision came during the greatest trial Louise and I had ever been through. The decision was whether or not to accept the wisdom of Josif Tson, who pulled no punches when I shared my hurt and bitter soul with him. This story is well known by those who have followed my ministry. This Romanian minister looked straight into my eyes one day and said, "R. T., you must totally forgive them. Until you totally forgive them you will be in chains. Release them and you will be released." No one had ever talked to me like that in my life. Faithful are the wounds of a friend (see Proverbs 27:6). That encounter with Josif Tson changed my life more than any word ever spoken to me. It not only set me free, but it paved the way for one hard decision after another from that day. It resulted in more insight than ever and is the true explanation for the books I have written, among them *God Meant It for Good* and the trilogy: *Total Forgiveness, Totally Forgiving Ourselves* and *Totally Forgiving God.*

The reason for referring to my "total forgiveness" experience with Josif is that—without knowing it—I was faced with the choice of whether to pursue or reject the fruit of the Spirit. I was at the crossroads that day. I was not happy with Josif's word. Josif himself recalls how angry I was. But I eventually took it in. It made all the difference. It came down to whether I truly wanted all of God I could have—which I had claimed—or not.

During that time I began preaching from the life of Joseph the son of Jacob. When I saw from Scripture how deeply and totally Joseph had forgiven his brothers (who were prepared to kill him), I was able to show whether or not I myself had truly forgiven people who had hurt me. The list of those I had to forgive grew almost daily! It meant: (1) not telling anybody what "they" did; (2) not letting these people feel afraid or nervous around me; (3) not pointing the finger or making them feel guilty; (4) letting them save face rather than "rubbing their noses in it"; (5) not revealing their darkest secret; (6) being prepared to forgive them every day for the rest of my life—this being a "life sentence"; and (7) blessing them, that is, sincerely asking God to bless them and not punish them. When Jesus commanded us to pray for our enemies He did not mean our saying, "Lord, I commit them to You"—which is a cop-out. He wants us to pray from our hearts that God will truly bless them.

I remember praying one day for someone who had done great emotional damage to one of our children, "Lord, bless them." Suddenly it seemed that the Lord came right back and said to me, "And suppose I *do* answer your prayer and bless them?" I thought, "Oh no, Lord, You wouldn't do that, would You?"

Oh yes, He would! And then I had to decide whether to keep praying on and on and on—every day—"Lord, bless them, bless them," or stop praying. It was hard at first to pray that God would truly bless certain people knowing He may well indeed answer my prayer. Then it became easier—until it ceased to be a problem at all. Why? Because I realized that if people prayed that way for *me—knowing how unworthy and undeserving I am*—perhaps God hearing my prayer for my enemies was an earnest prayer that God would bless me! Whereas I may feel they do not deserve to be prayed for like that, I ask: Do I? Do *I* deserve to be prayed for? The truthful answer is no. Absolutely not. I can tell you that God knows enough about me to bury me—to yank me out of the ministry at any time. I have continued by the sheer grace of God. No enemy of mine could be worse than I myself have been in God's sight.

The Key to All the Fruits of the Spirit

The first fruit of the Spirit mentioned is love. *Agape* love is always selfless concern; it is sacrificial caring, an unselfish motivation. It will allow the other person to save face. It is to carry out the Golden Rule, doing unto others as you would *wish* them to do to you (see Luke 6:31). It keeps no record of wrongs (see 1 Corinthians 13:5). We keep records to show that we have paid. We keep a record of wrongs with the intent of using what we know against others; to cause them to lose face, to remind them of their faults and to make them feel guilty. The fruit of the Spirit is love that *chooses* to overlook a multitude of sins. It is the love that motivated God to send His Son into the world to die on a cross for our sins (see John 3:16). It is utterly unselfish. But it is always a choice we make. Do not expect this love to flow automatically from you because you have the Holy Spirit. If *wisdom* was mentioned first because of its importance among the spiritual gifts, *love* is put at the head of the list when it comes to the fruit of the Spirit because it is the key to the fruits that follow. One should note: In the Greek it is the *fruit* not *fruits*, although that is not of crucial significance. "The fruit of the Spirit is love, joy, peace. . . ." To be *ambitious in love* is to forgive those who have hurt us—and to forgive them totally. The immediate result is joy and peace.

If, therefore, one truly excels in the love that is depicted in 1 Corinthians 13, he or she will possess and exude those virtues that Paul lists following that love: joy, peace, patience, kindness, goodness, faithfulness, gentleness and self-control. But love is a choice we must make. Were it not for the Holy Spirit in us we would not be able to make that choice. But with the Spirit we can. Once we move in love we experience the other fruits of the Spirit. In other words, all these qualities flow out of love. If you have love you will have joy; if you have love you will have patience; if you have love you will be kind, etc. But it begins by an act of the will.

So now—at last—we have approached the main point of this book! We are here right now. Are you ambitious? Then channel it in one direction: toward the glory and honor of God. Do you want to go for the gold? Then let the most difficult exercise, discipline, preparation and hardship be turned into one desire: *Pray for that person who has hurt you the most.* That abusive authority figure when you were a child. That unfair parent who never accepted you. That rapist. That unjust judge. That church leader who refused to recognize you. That authority figure who left you an emotional wreck. That racially biased person who walked all over you. That person who lied about you and ruined your reputation. That person who promised you a job but then gave it to someone else. That friend who betrayed you. That spouse who was unfaithful to you.

An Act of the Will

The greater the suffering, the greater the blessing and anointing that will be coming down the road to you—that is, if you *totally* forgive. Suffering is of no value, is absolutely worthless if you remain bitter. You may have thought that extreme suffering somehow elevates you to a level of entitlement; that God owes you certain things in life as compensation. I am sorry, but this is not the case. Your suffering has no merit until you get over your bitterness. The only way to do it is to forgive—and pray that God will bless those who have been so unkind and unfair. You may be the object of the worst injustice, the worst hurt and mistreatment; such is for nothing until you forgive and do so totally.

Total forgiveness—the proof of love—is a choice: It is an act of the will. It does not come automatically because you are a Christian. You do have the Holy Spirit because you are a Christian, yes (see Romans 8:9). But in order to demonstrate love—the first fruit of the Spirit that Paul mentioned—you must exercise discipline. Because you *are* a Christian you *can* do it. But it is a choice we all must make. Love keeps no record of wrongs, but you must *choose* whether you are going to tear up that record of wrongs or keep throwing them up to those people you want to play "Gotcha" with or get even with.

Moreover, love brings with it all the other fruits of the Spirit—joy, peace, patience, etc. This is because *agape* love is in itself patient, kind, does not envy, does not boast, is not proud, is not rude, is not self-seeking, is not easily angered. It "always protects, always trusts, always hopes, always perseveres" (1 Corinthians 13:4–7). Love is the key to the other fruits of the Spirit; it is the door that opens the way to those other sublime virtues. Aim for this love—pursue it with all your heart—and you will get the fruits of the Spirit thrown in.

Love, then, is first on the list when it comes to the *fruit* of the Spirit. If you want to be ambitious, here is your chance! It is an opportunity to be ambitious to the hilt—because you are going for the gold. This is godly ambition. This is ambition born in heaven. This is having an aspiration that is honoring to God.

Humility

If *agape* love is the key to the other fruits of the Spirit, humility is the sum total of them all. And yet it is like the old question: Which comes first, the chicken or the egg? Does love bring humility—or does humility lead to love? After all, when you totally forgive it means that your pride has been dealt a severe blow. It is our pride that will not let us admit we are wrong; it is humility that makes us choose to let hurtful people off the hook.

Humility is having a modest estimate of yourself—of your importance or rank. It is the opposite of arrogance or conceitedness. It is the willingness not to get the credit when in fact you deserve it. It is the grace not to take yourself so seriously. Humility is the identical twin of meekness. Indeed, one fruit of the Spirit is "meekness" (Galatians 5:23 KJV), "gentleness" in the New International Version. Meekness is that quality that enables you to accept an insult or criticism without fighting back or retorting. It is the opposite of defensiveness. It is turning the other cheek (see Matthew 5:39).

One of the main things about humility is that it does not elbow in on another's profile. It is being content with low or no profile at all. It is what characterizes the person who does not need to be the "head" or the "eye" in the Body of Christ, as we will see further below. Mind you, some people are happy to be "behind the scenes" anyway—not because they are truly humble but because they are made that way. Some people love the limelight; some do not. Those who love it and are willing *not* to be recognized are more likely to be truly humble; those who do not love the limelight should not make a big deal of it or their pride pops out after all!

When Paul dealt with spiritual gifts the issue of humility was never far away from his mind. When it comes to the motivational gifts we are admonished not to think of ourselves more highly than we ought to think (see Romans 12:3), and as soon as Paul dealt with the gifts of the Holy Spirit he embarked upon the subject of unity (see 1 Corinthians 12:12). The only way for unity to prevail in the Body of Christ is that everyone be filled with love and humility.

In other words, the fruit of the Spirit must match the gifts of the Spirit. It is not one or the other that is needed; we need both—equally. The gifts of the Spirit will inevitably lead to pride if they are not permeated with love and humility. We can be proud of our wisdom, conceited regarding our words of knowledge, vain about our prophetic gifts. I have been close to a number of people with prophetic gifts. I know how tempted some are to gloat if a prophecy comes true and how—in some cases—there is a rival spirit between prophetic people as to who has the greater gift. And since the spiritual gifts are "without repentance" there is the obvious need for humility.

Humility is not one of the *gifts* of the Spirit but is the essence of the *fruit* of the Spirit. Having stated that the Body is not made up of one part but of many, Paul asks, "If the foot should say, 'Because I am not a hand, I do not belong to the body,' it would not for that reason cease to be part of the body" (1 Corinthians 12:15). What is Paul's point? It is to show that some gifts or offices in the Body of Christ get more attention than others—but all are needed.

> The eye cannot say to the hand, "I don't need you!" And the head cannot say to the feet, "I don't need you!" On the contrary, those parts of the body that seem to be weaker [i.e. not visible as kidneys, intestines] are indispensable, and the parts that we think are less honorable we treat with special honor. And the parts that are unpresentable are treated with special modesty, while our presentable parts need no special treatment.
>
> verses 21–24

Why all this discussion? "So that there should be no division in the body" (verse 25).

We are all human. We are by nature prone to jealousy and pride. We naturally want the credit for what we do. We must learn to humble ourselves. One way to do it is to take the "lowest" seat rather than the place of honor when invited to a banquet. If we take the lowest seat it means humbling ourselves; if we choose the place of honor it could mean that God will humble us! Jesus gave the parable to show how those who are more distinguished may show up and you, having chosen a seat of honor, will have to sit elsewhere—and be embarrassed! Everyone who exalts himself will be humiliated; those who humble themselves will be exalted (see Luke 14:7–11).

The thesis of this book may be put in a sentence: that we will truly become ambitious to seek after the glory that comes from God alone and not from people. If people do not give you due credit for something you did, be glad! It is an opportunity you should *welcome and embrace* in order to say, "Lord, I want *Your approval*—nothing more." And if He does not appear to convey His approval, keep seeking it anyway without looking over your shoulder. Learn not to take seriously the compliments and praise of people. Keep focused on Jesus Christ alone—and His glory. That is the ambition that pleases God.

Unsanctified Ambition

Do nothing out of selfish ambition or vain conceit, but in humility consider others better than yourselves.

Philippians 2:3

Diotrephes, who loves to be first, will have nothing to do with us.

3 John 9

Dionysius to brother Novatian, greeting. If you were led on unwillingly, as you claim, then you can prove it by retreating willingly. One should endure anything rather than split the church of God, and martyrdom to avert schism I think more glorious than to avoid idolatry. For in the case of the latter one is martyred for the sake of his own single soul, but the former for the sake of the whole church.

Quoted by Eusebius (d. 339)

Truth is generally the best vindication against slander.

Abraham Lincoln (1809–1865)

There is nothing more promising for the Kingdom of God than godly ambition, and yet there is nothing worse and more threatening to the Church than unsanctified motivation. God bestows a higher level of motivation and ambition on some people in order to provide needed leadership, but it is a sad day in the Church when unholy motivation creeps into those who love prominence. Diotrephes was a threat to the unity of the Body of Christ in John's day. John summed it up: Diotrephes "loves to be first."

And yet does that not describe many of us? Most of us love to be first—whether standing in a queue, waiting for our names to be called, how well we do in sports, getting a good grade in taking a course or getting recognition for a job well done. As Dale Carnegie put it, the greatest drive of a human being is the desire to feel important. Indeed, significance is a normal desire for all of humanity. But if that desire is not held in check it can get out of hand and, possibly, ruin us. In honor we should prefer one another (see Romans 12:10), esteeming each other as being better than ourselves (see Philippians 2:3). Those of us who want to be Number One in everything—and want to be seen as the most important—are most vulnerable to the snares and temptations of the devil. We need to be sprinkled with the blood of Christ at all times and be sure that our ambition is sanctified. Never forget: The heart is deceitful (Jeremiah 17:9).

Schism

Unsanctified ambition is almost always the cause of disunity in the Church. The reason why Paul followed his discussion on the gifts of the Spirit by comparing the human body to the Body of Christ was for the sake of unity. Indeed, God has wisely placed people as they are where they are to avoid schism. "God has combined the members of the Body and has given greater honor to the parts that lacked it." In other words, God has taken our sense of significance and self-esteem into consideration when He created us, converted us and placed us in His Body. He spread out the gifts and talents in the Body of Christ that there would be minimal envy. He wants all of us to be honored. He has no problem with our being esteemed as long as we are not arrogant and God gets all the glory. After all, this is the way we are made. If each of us seeks to obtain God's honor we will be perfectly happy with the way we are made and where we are put in the Body. We are, therefore, given positions that fit both our needs and the Church's needs that "there should be no *division* in the body" (1 Corinthians 12:25, emphasis added; "schism," KJV). "Schism" is a better translation of the Greek word *schisma* that means "split, rend or tear apart." It may refer to a split between two strongly opposing parties or opinions.

Wherever you find division in the Church you may be sure that a bruised ego is not far away. "An offended brother is more unyielding than a fortified city" (Proverbs 18:19). A pastor needs to be a shrewd diplomat when shepherding his people, keeping in mind the fragile egos of this world. Paul wisely took this aspect of ministering into account. "I plead with Euodia and I plead with Syntyche to agree with each other in the Lord" (Philippians 4:2). Paul does not take sides. But he obviously appeals to two strong-willed women in the Church to make up. They must have caused a lot trouble for him to single them out by name. And why do you suppose Paul lists the names of no fewer than 26 people to whom he wants to be remembered—in Romans 16:1–16? It is because they deserve to be honored like that, and also because it will make each of them feel significant. But when you begin thanking people by name, woe to you (sometimes) if you leave someone's name out!

I have often wondered whether many theological controversies in Church history had nothing whatever to do with theology but with personality conflict. I think that when we get to heaven and get to see a DVD replay of the details of doctrinal controversies, we will be surprised if not shocked to see how much personal feeling and vendetta often had more to do with division than pure doctrine. I remember reading Cotton Mather's account of American Puritanism in which he noted that John Cotton, who founded Boston, and Thomas Hooker, who founded Connecticut, were two stars who simply could not stay in the same place together. It is the sort of thing that has characterized so much of Church history and doctrinal controversies. I think this would make a good Ph.D. thesis!

Follow Jesus' Example

The way forward for us all is to become more and more like Jesus. Having exhorted that we should in humility consider others better than ourselves, Paul made his case for maintaining unity of the church in Philippi by recalling Jesus' decision to leave the glory He had with the Father and become a man:

> Your attitude should be the same as that of Christ Jesus: who, being in very nature God, did not consider equality with God something to be grasped, but made himself nothing, taking the very nature of a servant, being made in human likeness. And being found in appearance as a man, he humbled himself and became obedient to death—even death on a cross!
>
> Philippians 2:5–8

I remember hearing a sermon in Nashville, Tennessee, in the spring of 1956 that had a most shattering effect on me. Dr. Hugh Benner took his text from Philippians 2:5–8—just quoted—and pointed out that when God became a man without ceasing to be God, He made himself of "no reputation" (KJV). Dr. Benner made the case that Jesus became the "lowest possible shame." Those were his words. That sermon for some reason drove me to my knees. I prayed a prayer I possibly should not have prayed. But I did; I asked God to make me the "lowest possible shame" in order that I might be like Jesus. I had no reason to believe at the time that this prayer would be answered. I was on top, riding high as a Trevecca student and Nazarene pastor, driving a new Chevrolet given to me by my grandmother, quite popular with nearly everybody and the "bright-eyed boy" of my denomination. But in a matter of a few months, having made some unpopular decisions, I displeased my father and nearly all my relatives. One of them actually said to me, "You are a disgrace. You are a shame to the family." My grandmother also took the car back. That might have hurt a lot except that I immediately recalled my prayer. It gave me no small comfort that I had uttered that prayer, although I am not sure a person should have prayed as I did. I do not recommend it. That said, I began an era of deep hurt, severe misunderstanding and great dilemma. It lasted for a long time.

In those days I became ambitious for vindication—mainly to be vindicated in the eyes of my dad. It was the first time in my life I felt a sense of rejection—from family and friends. No one seemed to believe in me. I will, however, never forget that my Grandpa McCurley said of me, "I'm for him right or wrong." I needed that kind of unconditional love.

I cannot say that my sense of ambition was curtailed or sanctified during those days. My motivation and ambition became all the greater and even more intense to prove to my dad that I had not gotten it wrong. Things went from bad to worse. Because of my unwise spending and enormous debts, I had to abandon any hope of a full-time ministry. That convinced my father I was truly out of the will of God. Selling vacuum cleaners door-to-door for the next several years did not help my case. But John 5:44 ("How can you believe if you accept praise from one another, yet make no effort to obtain the praise that comes from the only God?") was beginning to take seed in my mind. It was not easy. I did *not* achieve seeking only the honor of God in those days; neither do I say I have achieved it now. But the comforting thing about that unusual verse is that Jesus only implies that we should *make an attempt* to obtain His praise; *seek* the honor that comes from God only (KJV). The Pharisees, who missed their Messiah, made *no* attempt to seek the honor of God. Such a pursuit apparently did not cross their minds. In any case, I began a journey that has taken me to this day—seeking the honor that comes from God only—with all the ambition I can muster. I am still in pursuit of that glory.

Not seeking the honor that comes from God only is to fertilize the soil for unsanctified ambition.

Whose Side Is God On?

The problem is, nearly all who are a part of division or controversy would claim "God is on our side." In the American Civil War, both those of the North and the South felt equally they were fighting for the truth. The Labour Party in Great Britain was founded by Christians, but most Christians in England today vote with the Conservative Party. I have good evangelical friends in America who are Democrats, but most evangelicals are apparently Republicans. Both would honestly claim that God is on "their" side. We all feel God is on "our" side. I have marveled how Abraham Lincoln noted during the Civil War that he was not so concerned with whether God was on *his* side but whether he was on *God's* side, which showed an amazing objectivity in a time of horrible conflict.

What is the way forward? I believe it is to adopt the spirit of the apostle Paul, who was vehemently accused by his own converts in Corinth of getting it wrong. His reply:

> I care very little if I am judged by you or any human court; indeed, I do not even judge myself. My conscience is clear, but that does not make me innocent. It is the Lord who judges me. Therefore judge nothing before the appointed time; wait till the Lord comes. He will bring to light what is hidden in darkness and will expose the motives of men's hearts. At that time each will receive his praise from God.
>
> 1 Corinthians 4:3–5

Having to wait "till the Lord comes" is not a pleasant thing to hear when our flesh is crying out for our names to be cleared immediately. But it is the journey of waiting that makes all the difference. At one of my worst moments at Westminster Chapel my eyes fell on the words "God is just: He will pay back trouble to those who trouble you." *Oh, good!* I thought; that is, until I kept reading: "This will happen when the Lord Jesus is revealed from heaven in blazing fire with his powerful angels" (2 Thessalonians 1:6–7). Oh dear. I now realized I might have a long time to wait!

When Paul said that he did not even judge himself, he meant that he was not qualified to render a final verdict regarding himself; only God can do that. Paul must have judged himself in a sense or how could he know his conscience was clear? In the same epistle he said that the spiritual person judges all things (see 1 Corinthians 2:15). He also said that every person must judge himself or herself before partaking of the Lord's Supper (see 1 Corinthians 11:28–29). We all must make certain judgments and examinations along the way. So when he said that he did not even judge himself he meant that he was prepared to wait for God to reveal *His* infallible and final opinion regarding who was right and who was wrong.

The way forward, then, is to become ambitious in refusing to judge oneself or to make the claim "God is on our side." When Joshua saw the angel as he entered the land of Canaan he asked, "Are you for us or for our enemies?" I do not think Joshua was prepared for the reply: "Neither." Joshua obediently and submissively took off his shoes; he was on holy ground. We must all take off our shoes, refusing to point the finger at those who oppose us. God will show whose side He is on in His time. Until then we are not to claim to be in the right—even if our consciences are clear; we must wait for God to step in. While we wait we can worship. While we wait we can seek the honor that comes from God only. While we wait we can cultivate an ambition that shows we are not trying to prove ourselves. This quest brings liberty and joy. The greatest freedom is having nothing to prove.

Controlling the Tongue

One of the noblest ambitions you and I can have is to control our tongues. It is also the greatest challenge on earth. It is comforting that James tells us that no one can tame the tongue and that we all stumble in many ways (see James 3:2, 8). But sadly that does not let us off the hook! We are responsible for our words. My most "unfavorite" verse in the Bible is Matthew 12:36, the words of Jesus: "I tell you that men will have to give account on the day of judgment for every careless word they have spoken." Oh dear.

It is the lack of tongue control that gets us into trouble. Wisdom will lead us to control what we say, and yet controlling what we say also leads us to godly wisdom. If 1 Corinthians 13 is the "love" chapter of the Bible and Hebrews 11 the "faith" chapter, James 3 is the "tongue" chapter. As we will see below, James concludes his discussion of taming the tongue by showing two kinds of wisdom: (1) that which is from below and (2) wisdom that comes from heaven. Back to the old question: Which comes first, the chicken or the egg? So does tongue control lead to wisdom or does wisdom lead to controlling our words?

One thing is certain: If we harbor bitter envy and selfish ambition in our hearts, there will be no grace to control the tongue. Bitter envy means unforgiveness and holding a grudge. Selfish ambition is manifested when you demand recognition because you think you deserve the credit. But be careful. Count on it if we think we are not getting enough credit: Venom will spew from our lips like an active volcano that cannot be controlled. What erupts from our deceitful hearts will be "earthy, unspiritual, of the devil" and is instantly recognizable by *selfish ambition* (James 3:15–16). But wisdom that is from heaven is pure, peace-loving, considerate, submissive, full of mercy and good fruit, impartial and sincere (see James 3:17). It is disdaining selfish ambition—that is, seeing it in ourselves and disavowing it—that we must sincerely strive for. The wisdom that comes from above, namely, the presence of the mind of the Holy Spirit, will help spare us of regret when it comes to our words. It brings us back to total forgiveness and the vow to stop pointing the finger.

In the light of the teaching of "total forgiveness," do we not have to judge another person now and then? No. We do not *have* to do so. But it is not easy. It is hard not to let your right hand know what your left hand is doing—meaning, I do not even tell myself if I give to the poor (see Matthew 6:3); but it is a noble ambition to pursue such a goal. We must never keep a record of wrongs in our hearts—not to mention verbally pointing the finger; we must equally never keep a record of *rights*—that is, pompously claiming to have got it right. If I am not to judge myself because this is God's prerogative, I must also make it my aim not to judge another. It is, simply, not my right (see Matthew 7:1). But I cannot imagine a greater ambition!

I am sometimes asked, "How do you discipline people in the Church when they obviously need it? Aren't you judging them?" Answer: This is different. The reason is because such a judgment is not personal. The need to exercise discipline in the Church must never be personal; that is, you are not trying to get even. I had a case in which a church member was sleeping with another man's wife. I told him that he must stop it or immediately resign his membership. He refused to stop sinning and vowed to let the church deal with this. Mercifully he resigned his membership only hours before the church meeting. There is nothing personal in Church discipline; it is to keep cancer in the Body from spreading.

Outside the Church

The issue of unsanctified ambition is not limited to the Church. You may be a lawyer and want to have a larger practice. You may be a secretary who wants a promotion. You may be in business and aspire to make a lot of money. The principle is the same with the Christian in the world as it is in the Church. You make a choice whether to let God promote you or to manipulate your way to the top. You will ask: How do you know it is God promoting you when you have an opportunity to step in and make things happen? I reply: When an opportunity falls into your lap, chances are this is from God. But wait. Here are five principles one can live by to avoid becoming carnally ambitious. Follow the acrostic PEACE: Providential, Enemy, Authority, Confidence, Ease. Ask these questions when you are faced with an opportunity or decision:

Is it *providential*? Does a door open up or do you have to knock it down?

What do you suppose the *enemy* (Satan) would have you do? Do the opposite and you will get it right.

What does your *authority* (the Bible) have to say regarding this? Is there Scripture against what you might do? Does the Bible support it?

Does your *confidence* increase or diminish (it should increase)? The more I know I am in God's will, the more confidence I have.

Do you have *ease* in making this decision? To quote Shakespeare: "To thine own self be true." What do you feel in your heart of hearts?

You need *all five* of the above to be sure you are proceeding without unsanctified ambition. Chances are, if all five of these cohere, you are being safely led and are not being deceived.

To summarize: Do the things that make for peace (see Romans 14:19)—both externally and internally. Externally, does your decision make others feel this is right and fair? Internally, do you have peace in your heart about this? God will never lead you in a direction by which you lose peace in your heart.

Unsanctified ambition causes havoc in the Church and destroys lives outside the Church. Unsanctified ambition leads to burnout, nervous breakdowns, broken marriages, ill health, sleeplessness, losing friends and—sometimes—losing money. Living by the principles of the glory of God will lead you safely in the direction you should go. Which would you prefer—to be promoted to the level of your incompetence in order to get prestige and glory by your own efforts, or for God to promote you? Do you honestly want what is not best for you? God has a better idea than you have for what is best. Do not deprive Him of letting Him exalt you in due time (see 1 Peter 5:6). His best is worth waiting for.

God has a plan for your life. He only wants what is best for you. He will never promote you to the level of your incompetence. You will never forfeit the best when, in fact, He is the One who wants the best for you. No good thing will He withhold from you if you follow His honor for your life (see Psalm 84:11).

Ambition and Vindication

"Come, let us build ourselves a city, with a tower that reaches to the heavens, so that we may make a name for ourselves and not be scattered over the face of the whole earth."

Genesis 11:4

During his lifetime Absalom had taken a pillar and erected it in the King's Valley as a monument to himself, for he thought, "I have no son to carry on the memory of my name."

2 Samuel 18:18

Regard your good name as the richest jewel you can possibly be possessed of—for credit is like fire; when once you have kindled it you may easily preserve it, but if you once extinguish it, you will find it an arduous task to rekindle it again. The way to gain a good reputation is to endeavor to be what you desire to appear.

Socrates (469 BC–399 BC)

Who steals by purse steals trash; 'tis something, nothing;
'Twas mine, 'tis his, and has been slave to thousands;
But he who filches from me my good name
Robs me of that which not enriches him
And makes me poor indeed.

William Shakespeare (1564–1616)

In Hollywood they say that it does not matter what people, reviews or the press reveals about you as long as they spell your name correctly. But that is Hollywood—where integrity or morals do not matter.

Any ambition on our part to make a name for ourselves will be brought to light at the Judgment Seat of Christ when the "true truth" (to use Francis Schaeffer's phrase) will be unveiled. That truth will include whether or not we tried to make ourselves look good—that is, whether or not God did it—and what was absolutely true about each of us. Any effort to "make a name" for ourselves is to move in on God's territory. He is not pleased with our doing that. It is like trying to vindicate ourselves. Vindication is what God does. It is also what He does best, but He only vindicates the *truth*. "It is mine to avenge" (Romans 12:19). He is, however, jealous for your reputation and mine. He is also jealous for His own glory. Like it or not, that is the way He is. He is certainly grieved when we needlessly ruin our reputations by sin or sheer stupidity. But He will not bend the rules for any of us.

If, therefore, God's glory is what lies behind our motivation and ambition, our reputation will take care of itself. He delights in our good name if He is the One who made it. So if you and I live for *His* glory, our reputation or good name becomes His responsibility. We do not need to be concerned with what people think. I have carried a newspaper clipping in my wallet for more than sixty years; it is advice that former United States President James Garfield (1831–1881) was given—and which he had carried in his wallet most of his life until he was assassinated:

- Make few promises.
- Always speak the truth.
- Live within your income.
- Never speak evil of anyone.
- Keep good company or none.
- Keep your own secrets, if you have any.
- Never borrow, if you can possibly avoid it.
- Keep yourself honest, if you would be happy.
- When you speak to a person, look into his eyes.
- Make no haste to be rich, if you would prosper.
- Save when you are young, to spend when you are old.
- Never run into debt, unless you see a way out again.
- If anyone speaks evil of you, let your life be so that no one will believe it.
- Your character cannot be hurt except by your own deeds.

The Tower of Babel

One of the first signs of ambition in the Bible was the motivation in those people who built the tower of Babel. They did it "so that we may make a name for ourselves." Their motivation to make a *name* is what got God's attention. He stepped in and said, "Come, let us go down and confuse their language so they will not understand each other." The Lord scattered them from there over all the earth, and they stopped building the city (see Genesis 11:4–8).

We should learn from this that making a name for ourselves is a wrong kind of ambition. It is one thing for ambition to drive us to service, as Martin Luther allegedly put it, quite another to be motivated by our self-esteem and pride, as implied in Ecclesiastes 4:4. We must also be wary of trying to make things happen. We must not pursue something that God did not initiate in the first place. God wants to be the One who initiates things and makes things happen.

He will make things happen—if we will let Him—but only the things that are best for us. I know what it is to get it badly wrong regarding pressing toward a goal without knowing whether or not it was God's will. This could refer to anything from pushing an idea, planning a trip, having a conversation, writing a book or accepting an invitation. I also know what it is to be reprimanded when I would work behind the scenes to meet someone who is famous, well connected and able to enhance my reputation. And one of the worst things in this connection is to engineer a prestigious invitation.

I tried a thousand ways, for example, to meet Nelson Mandela. I regard him as the greatest person who ever lived outside the Bible and Church history. Moreover, you would not believe the number of people who were apparently close to him who said, "Leave it with me. I can set that up." During one of my first trips to South Africa—on a flight to Cape Town where I was to meet with his closest aide—my eyes fell on Jeremiah 45:5: "Should you then seek great things for yourself? Seek them not." That sobering verse hit me right between the eyes. I will never forget it as long as I live. I could take you virtually to the same seat where I was on the plane. I stopped my pursuit after that and asked that those who were working on this also to stop it. Although I could make a case that I wanted to do this for the glory of God, I knew in my heart of hearts that my motive at bottom was selfish and self-seeking. Would I be willing to meet President Mandela if no one would hear about it? Perhaps, but it would be very hard to keep quiet about it. My ambition to meet him in any case was not motivated by the Holy Spirit. I hope I have learned a lesson from this.

"No one from the east or the west or from the desert can exalt a man. But it is God who judges: He brings one down, he exalts another" (Psalm 75:6–7). God will honor us for being non-manipulative when it comes to our reputation.

But there is, then, another equally important matter connected to this—vindication. Do not deprive God of doing what is His prerogative alone—and what He does best. Vindication is like salvation; God wants all the glory. When Jesus died on the cross it was a way of showing the whole world that we are saved by *what God's Son did, not what we can do.* The story of redemption is one continual demonstration of the sovereign grace of God. None of us—no exceptions—can get any glory from the fact that we are Christians. All the glory goes to God—forever and ever. Jesus not only died for us but carries out the Father's will in such a manner that all the glory—*all of it*—goes to Him. Our salvation is based upon God's electing grace (He chose us from the foundation of the world), His effectual calling (the Holy Spirit quickens us, giving us faith to believe) and keeping us saved (see Romans 8:30). So, too, with vindication. If you and I tamper with clearing our names and making ourselves look good we elbow in on God's territory. He does not like that one bit. My loving and firm counsel: Leave it to God when it comes to having your name cleared.

Rebekah and Jacob

We saw earlier that God appealed to Abraham's innate desire for significance when He promised to make Abraham's name "great" (see Genesis 12:1ff). Abraham was the prototype Christian in the Old Testament—showing for example how we are justified by faith (see Genesis 15:6), how we should tithe (see Genesis 14:18–20), how we respond to the call for perfection (see Genesis 17) and—last but not least—how we experience God swearing an oath to us (see Genesis 22).

We also observed that Moses was motivated by reward. He left the palace of Pharaoh because he was able to see beyond the pleasures of sin. He consciously chose the reward that would be coming down the road (see Hebrews 11:24). Although he initially jumped the gun in trying to impress his brothers who were suffering, God later sorted him out and Moses became the greatest man of the Old Testament.

In a word: Abraham and Moses were examples of healthy ambition.

Not so with Jacob and his mother, Rebekah. Neither was a shining example of sanctified ambition. Esau was the firstborn and his father, Isaac, was partial to him from the beginning. But Jacob was Rebekah's favorite. The firstborn in ancient times received double the inheritance. The cunning Jacob seemed to have had his eye on Esau's birthright from early days. Jacob seized the moment when Esau came home one day thinking he was starving to death. When Esau begged for food Jacob said okay—but first give me your birthright. Esau reckoned he was dying anyway so he agreed (see Genesis 25:29–34).

But there was more. When it was time for their father, Isaac, to give the patriarchal blessing, Jacob—following his mother's crafty counsel—pretended successfully to be Esau. Isaac, who was blind, fell for the scheme and pronounced his supreme and coveted blessing upon Jacob (see Genesis 27:27–29). Esau then protested and Isaac recognized what Jacob had done. Furthermore, Isaac is given a place in Hebrews 11 for sticking to his guns after realizing he had been deceived—pronouncing that Jacob, though he was the trickster, "will be blessed" (see Genesis 27:33; Hebrews 11:20). Rebekah and Jacob got what they were ambitious for. Esau, however, is later called "godless" and is cited as an example of an inability to find repentance (Hebrews 12:16–17; see also Hebrews 6:4–6).

An Eternal Mystery

It is in this story of Jacob and Esau—possibly more than any other account in the entire Bible—that we are faced with the eternal mystery pertaining to the sovereignty of God and man's role. Was it carnal ambition that actually achieved Jacob's (and Rebekah's) goal? Or was it rather the fulfillment of the prophetic word to Rebekah that preceded the twins' births—"The older shall serve the younger"—that motivated both of them? Rebekah could never forget this word spoken by the Lord to her. In what manner God spoke to her is also a mystery. We are only told, "The LORD said to her, 'Two nations are in your womb, and two peoples from within you will be separated; one people will be stronger than the other, and the older will serve the younger'" (Genesis 25:23).

This same prophetic word to Rebekah was referred to by Paul when he observed that "before the twins were born or had done anything good or bad—in order that God's purpose in election might stand. . . . 'Jacob I loved, but Esau I hated'" (Romans

9:11). This means that God had determined the outcome, namely, that Esau would bow to Jacob. But this did not apparently happen apart from the rather questionable efforts of Rebekah and Jacob! And yet were not Rebekah and Jacob carrying out what was decreed? If so, are they to be blamed for mischievous ambition? Or was it rather a case of Rebekah and Jacob doing what they *wanted* to achieve while unconsciously carrying out God's sovereign will? I will not try further to solve this recondite issue in my book on ambition. But I must observe that God certainly used ambition to fulfill what had been decreed.

Ambition and King David

There is no indication that David was an ambitious man—that is, before he was anointed to be king by Samuel (see 1 Samuel 16:13). But that motivation lay hidden in his heart all the time, only waiting to be tapped. There are many like this; they do not feel ambitious. They have no reason to reach out for a realistic goal or to accept a challenge that would appear rewarding. In my teenage years I did not expect to make all As as I had once done; too many students around me were the bright ones, the "teacher's pets" and brimming over with self-confidence. It did not cross my mind to be voted "most likely to succeed" (as some were), to be invited to join the most popular club or to be president of my class. To come into one's own regarding motivation and ambition, there normally must be a measure of probability that one will succeed.

Samuel the prophet had been instructed to go to the house of Jesse to anoint one of his sons to be king. But David, the youngest of these sons, was not invited to meet Samuel. David was not on his father's radar screen. David's brothers had queued up before the legendary prophet—each no doubt hoping to be chosen for the kingship. It was only because Samuel insisted that Jesse send for David—who was a shepherd—that he was brought in from the sheep pens. To everyone's amazement, David was chosen to be the next king. And so it was utterly and totally out of David's hands.

But sometime after being anointed things changed. David was instructed by Jesse to see how his brothers were doing. They were in a battle against the Philistines, who were led by the giant Goliath. Once David heard what the reward was for killing Goliath, namely, great wealth, exemption from taxes plus marriage to the king's daughter (see 1 Samuel 17:25), David acted quickly. He volunteered to King Saul to kill Goliath. He turned out to have a double dose of ambition but which would be used for the glory of God. He said to Goliath, "I come against you in the name of the LORD Almighty, the God of the armies of Israel, whom you have defied" (1 Samuel 17:45). After David killed Goliath, King Saul became jealous of him. For the next twenty years David would use all the motivation in him—from the crown of his head to the soles of his feet—to stay alive. That same ambition and drive, therefore, motivated David over and over again in his hiding from Saul.

But there is more. That same drivenness in David became channeled in one direction—to glorify God. At some point in his pilgrimage, David narrowed all his desires down to one. Psalm 27:4 is the key to understanding David—throughout his life: "One thing I ask of the LORD, this is what I seek: that I may dwell in the house of the LORD all the days of my life, to gaze upon the beauty of the LORD and to seek him in his temple." This verse puts in bold relief the thesis of this book, namely, that all motivation and ambition in us should coalesce into one: to please God. And that was David. Whatever defects that emerged in him later on in his life, David was focused on God; he had a heart after God.

There are two halves of the life of David: (1) his pre-kingship era—during which he spent his time trying to stay alive by running from Saul; and (2) his life as king of Judah and Israel. In his pre-kingship days he had two opportunities to kill Saul (see 1 Samuel 24, 26) and refused. He demonstrated a greater aspiration to wait on God's timing rather than hasten his becoming the king. This, indeed, showed the greatness of David prior to the kingship. "Either [Saul's] time will come and he will die, or he will go into battle and perish. But the LORD forbid that I should lay a hand on the LORD's anointed" (1 Samuel 26:10–11). That same spirit governed David during his exile after he was king. In his darkest hour—when his son Absalom had seized the kingship—David counseled Zadok to take the revered Ark of the Covenant back to Jerusalem. David might have understandably wanted to keep the Ark at his side. But no. "If I find favor in the LORD's eyes he will bring me back and let me see it and his dwelling place again. But if he says, 'I am not pleased with you,' then I am ready; let him do to me whatever seems good to him" (2 Samuel 15:25–26). David knew that if he had vindication coming, he would be vindicated. He was prepared to let God decide. I repeat: God only vindicates the truth. David's example during his exile is the quintessence of sanctified ambition. It also meant that vindication in his case was only a matter of time.

David had an ambition to do what had never been done—to conquer Jerusalem. No one had succeeded in this—ever—owing to the topography of the area. To accomplish this he threw out a challenge to those strong men around him. The Jebusites, who had controlled Jerusalem, had said to David, "You will not get in here; even the blind and the lame can ward you off" (2 Samuel 5:6). David gets the credit for taking Jerusalem but, in fact, accomplished this by appealing to the sense of ambition of those around him. "Whoever leads the attack on the Jebusites will become commander-in-chief." It was an offer that Joab could not refuse: Joab "went up first" and so received this prestigious command (1 Chronicles 11:6).

David had become consumed with another ambition: to build the first Temple for the Lord. He received a premature encouragement to get on with this by the prophet Nathan. But God immediately slapped Nathan's wrist for jumping the gun and told the prophet that David was *not* to be the person to build the Temple. It was a huge disappointment for the king, but David's motivation to please the Lord won out. David accepted Nathan's verdict that it would be David's son—but not David—who would build the Temple (see 2 Samuel 7).

Unholy Ambition

Here follow several biblical examples.

Absalom

Earlier in this book we observed the folly of Absalom, who built a monument to himself. Absalom was an example of vile ambition. He played into the feelings of the people while King David seemed to be detached from what was going on. The Absaloms of this world today—small men with huge and selfish ambitions—are scattered in churches all over the world. These are often Number Two men who want to be Number One. They endear themselves ruthlessly to innocent people—to turn them away from God's man. We should thank God for godly Number Two men who do not have vain ambitions. So Absalom said to the people, "If only I were appointed judge in the land!" He exploited David's detachment from the people and their sense of need and, consequently, "stole the hearts of the men of Israel" (2 Samuel 15:1–6). Sadly, King David and his son Absalom were polar opposites when it comes to ambition. The king was a man after God's own heart; Absalom a man governed by unbridled ambition. These two men are perhaps best described by Jesus' words: "Whoever exalts himself will be humbled, and whoever humbles himself will be exalted" (Matthew 23:12).

Miriam and Aaron

Here are two people who were overcome by unholy ambition. They were jealous of Moses' calling and authority, so they opposed him. God stepped in and vindicated Moses by causing Miriam to become a leper. She became as white as snow, but Moses interceded for her and she was restored (see Numbers 12). There is nothing so sad and disruptive for a church leader to have ambitious people in the congregation or on the staff. But God will, sooner or later, bring the truth to bear and vindicate in His own time.

Adonijah

God had promised that Solomon would be king after David. But an ambitious man called Adonijah had other thoughts. He wanted to steal the kingdom. Unholy ambition seized him and he conspired to overthrow David's wish. He managed to persuade some of David's friends—Joab and Abiathar the priest—to keep Solomon from inheriting the kingdom. Sometimes an ambitious person can be cunning and lure good people away from God's will. The apostle John warned: "Watch out that you do not lose what you have worked for, but that you may be rewarded fully" (2 John 8). I know what it is for sincere Christians to be diverted from a straight course by carnal people. Adonijah was full of arrogance and pride, an enemy who wanted dominion. But Nathan the prophet and Bathsheba intervened and—in the nick of time—persuaded the aged and ailing King David to step in and make sure that Solomon got the throne (see 1 Kings 1:5–35). God is never too early, never too late, but always just on time.

Rehoboam

Possibly an even more blatant exhibition of carnal ambition in the Old Testament was in the case of Rehoboam, Solomon's son. The people pleaded with their new king to lighten their load a bit. This would have been an opportunity for Rehoboam to become a great hero. But Rehoboam's ambition to be seen as his own man won out. His pitiful ambition proved to be stronger than his father's wisdom. He wanted to be the greatest king of all but became one of the smallest men in Israelite history. The new king replied: "My little finger is thicker than my father's waist"—and decreed to make their load heavier than ever (1 Kings 12:10). It was a turning point in Rehoboam's kingship and the precipitating cause for the eventual downfall of Israel, leading to the division of the two kingdoms. Unsanctified ambition is not only dangerous but an easy tool for Satan to use to divide God's people.

Ananias and Sapphira

In the New Testament a couple whose names were Ananias and Sapphira aspired to be very "in" with the early Church. They were a part of the earliest Church. They were accepted as believers.

But greed crept into their hearts. There was a spontaneous move of the people to sell all their properties and lay all the money at the apostles' feet to be distributed among the poor. There was no requirement to do this; it was spontaneous and voluntary. Ananias and Sapphira would have been wise to keep at a distance and let those who felt led to sell their possessions do so. But they wanted to be seen as doing what so many were doing. They pretended to have sold their possessions and given all the money to the apostles.

Had there not been such a powerful presence of God on the scene in the earliest Church, Ananias and his wife may well have gotten away with their nefarious ambition to be accepted among the godly who were so transparent. But since God was so powerfully present as He was then, such deception was transmitted to Peter in an instant. I have frequently wondered if that kind of power would one day return to the Church were God to manifest His presence in great measure? If so, how many of us would truly *want* revival? Peter said to Ananias, "How is it that Satan has so filled your heart that you have lied to the Holy Spirit and have kept for yourself some of the money you received for the land? . . . What made you think of doing such a thing? You have not lied to men but to God" (Acts 5:3–4). Ananias was immediately struck dead. Sapphira repeated the same lie before Peter and she, too, was struck dead. Such judgment like this comes not on the lost but those truly saved. "When we are judged by the Lord, we are being disciplined so that we will not be condemned with the world" (1 Corinthians 11:32).

An Ambitious Mother

The mother of James and John asked Jesus to grant that her two sons be allowed to sit at His right and left hand when He came into His Kingdom. This came from a caring, loving but ambitious mother (see Matthew 20:20–21), but it is also possible that they put her up to it. Indeed, according to Mark's account the issue came up (or came up again) when the disciples were arguing on the way into Capernaum who should be the greatest (see Mark 9:33ff). In Luke's account this issue actually came up (or came up yet again) in one of the holiest moments of all—when Jesus was introducing Holy Communion—the Lord's Supper (see Luke 22:24). It is amazing how carnal thoughts do not disappear at holiest places and times! As Jeremiah said, the heart is deceitful above all things and desperately wicked; who can know it? (Jeremiah 17:9). The ambition to be right at the top when Jesus came into His Kingdom was never far away from the disciples' minds from the moment they became followers of Jesus. Even after Jesus had explained that the Kingdom of God does not come by observation but is "within" us (Luke 17:21), they did not grasp what He was saying. Jesus' answer was always the same: The greatest is not the one who is served but the one who serves (Matthew 20:26–27).

Not Necessarily a Sin

Josif Tson has pointed out, however, that Jesus never rebuked the disciples for their ambition to be great. This is important to remember. It is not a sin to be ambitious. It is not a virtue to be ambitious. It is how this ambition is used that makes the difference. Jesus showed His disciples the *way to greatness*, namely, by being servants. By becoming like a child. God uses ambition to drive us to service. Yes. But the service that pleases God is when we are true servants. He that wants to be first must be a slave (see Matthew 20:27). If indeed you and I do not become true slaves of Jesus Christ, sooner or later we will likely be put in the same position in which Jesus put Peter. When Jesus spoke of how Peter would die, Jesus prophesied to him: "When you were younger you dressed yourself and went where you wanted; but when you are old you will stretch out your hands, and someone will dress you and lead you where you do not want to go" (John 21:18). God has a way of sorting us out as we get older, driving us to the kind of ambition that truly honors the Most High God.

The way forward is to be sure that our greatest goal in life is to receive the praise that comes from God—not people. If we seek the praise of people, we may succeed, but we forfeit the praise and honor that would have come from God. If we seek the praise from God, sometimes God throws in some compliments from people. But the worst thing we can do is to let their praises mean too much to us—and begin to look for them. It is not unlike the word of Charles Spurgeon: "I looked to Christ and the Dove flew in; I looked to the Dove and he disappeared."

Too Much Ambition?

If you find honey, eat just enough—too much of it, and you will vomit.

Proverbs 25:16

Do you not know that your body is a temple of the Holy Spirit, who is in you, whom you have received from God? You are not your own; you were bought at a price. Therefore honor God with your body.

1 Corinthians 6:19–20

If, in a few months, I'm only Number Eight or Number Ten in the world, I'll have to look at what off-the-court work I can do. I will need to do something if I am to be Number One.

John McEnroe (b. 1959)

My father taught me one important lesson: not to be afraid to lose.

Chris Evert (b. 1954)

John McEnroe, who won seven Grand Slam singles titles in tennis (three at Wimbledon, four at the U.S. Open), was once the player everybody loved to hate. He shouted at umpires when receiving a bad call, *"You cannot be serious!"* and said to another, "Over one thousand officials to choose from and I get a moron like you." The crowds at Wimbledon gave him a hard time. But he claimed that Princess Diana watched him play at Wimbledon and pulled him aside to say, "I really feel for you."

So did I. I was always on edge when I watched him play. I almost felt as though I was in John McEnroe's skin. When he was cautioned by the umpire, I was afraid he would shout back. He usually did. When he lost his temper I said to myself, *That's me.* I cannot say I actually prayed for him when he played, but I almost did. I took it personally when he won, lost or shouted. It is said he was driven unmercifully by his army sergeant father from a child to excel, especially in tennis.

I, too, was driven by my well-meaning dad to excel—in anything. I suspect that—at bottom—he wanted me to do what he did not or could not do. I discovered his own report card one day. He made only Cs in school. As I said earlier, I was motivated to make the highest grades. The very highest. A-plus. Anything less than an A was devastating. When I presented my first essay at my Seminary in Louisville, Kentucky, I got an A-minus. I challenged my professor; he said if I had not split an infinitive I would have made an A. I stopped splitting infinitives from that day on.

I think a person can have too much ambition, certainly at the natural level. A person can have more ambition than intelligence, more motivation than needed in order to accomplish realistic goals. According to the Peter Principle, a person can be promoted to the level of his incompetence; too much ambition is often the culprit. I myself may have been given an overdose of ambition, but I do not believe the Holy Spirit ever promotes us to the level of our incompetence. We may promote ourselves beyond the prevenient work of the Spirit by running ahead of Him, but if we keep in step with Him we will not ever be ashamed.

In Pursuit of Self-Understanding

Do bear with me if I further bring you in on my own struggle in this area. I do so for one reason: in order that you can identify with those of us who have an overdose of ambition—whether you are an ambitious person or not—to the extent you, too, might gain a measure of self-understanding that will help set you free.

I was brought up as an only child. My sister, Marilyn, came along when I was fifteen. She could write my biography and call it "My Brother Was an Only Child," for that is the way I was raised—and the way she must feel. Had I had a brother or sister when I was very young it would almost certainly have made a difference in how I was raised. But I was the sole focus of my parents and grandparents. It led to my self-centeredness and—owing largely to my dad—drivenness.

But there was another factor—my aforementioned theological background. I was brought up to believe in sinless perfection. Most Nazarenes today would disavow that their understanding of Wesleyan teaching was sinless perfectionist. But to me it was certainly that. When I lost my temper at the age of *six*, burning my tongue on hot oatmeal before it cooled off—and shouting to my mother, "Why do you make things so hot?"—she replied: "If you got sanctified the Lord would take that bad temper out of you." The thing is, she really believed that. Such a comment made me all the more upset, angry, confused and frustrated. All my life I have fought against a hair-trigger temper. As Dr. Clyde Narramore put it, "As the twig is bent, so grows the tree." My goal of perfection so far has not been reached.

In 1970, as I have mentioned, I left my church in Fort Lauderdale to return to Trevecca to get my A.B. Immediately after that I entered Southern Baptist Theological Seminary in Louisville in January 1971, receiving the M.Div. in less than two years and the M.A. from the University of Louisville in June 1973. During those years I was pastor of the Blue River Baptist Church in Salem, Indiana—a forty-minute drive back and forth each day—for two and a half years. In September 1973 we moved to England for me to pursue the D.Phil. at Oxford. From 1974–1976, I was also pastor of the Calvary Baptist Church in Lower Heyford, Oxfordshire.

My years pursuing higher education were consumed with one thing—finishing well at Oxford. In the summer of 1975 my family and I took a vacation in Switzerland. The drive from Geneva to Interlaken without doubt provides one of the most spectacular views of green hills, Swiss chalets, lakes, flowing streams and snowcapped mountains of any place in the entire world. The four of us made that exact trip. But after it was over I did not remember a single thing. My mind was preoccupied with my research at Oxford—and getting that degree. I vaguely recall taking some photos with the kids. But my focus was elsewhere. By the time I learned that I had passed my oral exam at Oxford, I had accepted a call to Westminster Chapel. The same drivenness characterized my pastorate for 25 years there. I vaguely recall the children. In my book *Totally Forgiving Ourselves* I tell how I have had to forgive myself for my neglect—and I actually *have* done this.

But, sadly (here is the worst part), I have not really changed. That is, I am still as driven as ever—preaching and writing—with both of our children now married. Louise travels with me most places and she is a few feet away as I write these lines. But I have not really changed. Can a leopard change its spots?

Can a person have too much natural ambition? Yes. I am, therefore, describing myself at 77. At the moment I am in New Hampshire at a conference where I speak every year. In the previous two weeks I have flown from Seattle to Maine, then to London (for three days), back to Connecticut, then to Dallas, on to Sarasota and now New Hampshire. Between preaching—in hotels and on planes—I have worked on this very book. I am trying to cut down. A friend has recently cautioned me, "Your body is the temple of the Holy Spirit." Wherever I go they say, "You must cut down." But when I am in heaven I will not be able to write books—probably my main legacy. So should I not keep this up?

Am I describing a strength or a weakness? Is such motivation a virtue or a vice? Or is it both? Without this drive would I have returned to the university to get my A.B. in 1970? Probably not. Would I have been better off had I stayed in my church in Fort Lauderdale? Probably not. Would I have been better off not to have come to England? Who knows? If I had not come to England, I would not have been invited to Westminster Chapel. Would I—or they—have been better off had I not come? You tell me. Without my drive could I have preached some *four times a week* (all different sermons) in London for 25 years? Certainly not. Without this motivation could I continue to write two books a year? No. One thing I am sure of: Had I put my family first during those days in London I would have preached just as well, but I cannot get those years back. But what is my responsibility now? I have many open doors to present a message I would go to the stake for. Cannot I rest when I get to heaven?

These are questions I am asking in my old age.

Jacob

When I was young I identified with Joseph. My book *God Meant It for Good* is about Joseph. But in my old age I identify mostly with Joseph's driven father, Jacob. My book *All's Well That Ends Well* is about Jacob—the arch manipulator. In the previous chapter we looked at Jacob and his mother, Rebekah. After conspiring with his mother to get the patriarchal blessing from his father, Isaac, Jacob left home—fearing that Esau would kill him. But God was with Jacob and powerfully revealed His glory to him. Encouraged by a sense of God's presence (see Genesis 28:10–17), Jacob continued his journey and came into contact with a beautiful woman named Rachel, daughter of Laban.

Jacob fell head-over-heels in love with Rachel. He agreed happily to work for her father, Laban, for seven years in order to marry her. But after the night of the wedding—which took place by sleeping with her in a tent—he woke up and saw he had slept with Rachel's sister, Leah! Laban replied in so many words, "Sorry about that, Jacob, but we have a custom that the oldest daughter gets married first," then added: "I will give you Rachel if you work for me for another seven years." Jacob did—and finally got her (see Genesis 29:16–30).

One thing is fairly certain. Jacob got his drivenness *not* from his father but from his mother, Rebekah. The fear of Esau drove him away from home, and yet his strong motivation plus his vision from God are what helped him to survive the unjust carryings on by his father-in-law, Laban. Did Jacob have too much drivenness? Possibly not. It was the natural explanation for not giving up on Rachel—and is what lay behind his extreme patience with Laban. Was he foolish in letting Laban walk all over him as he did? Perhaps. Jacob's determination to get Rachel was so potent, however, that those years seemed like nothing. And Laban was utterly ruthless in business with Jacob over the years. Jacob had met his match. Having been a conniver and trickster over the years, Jacob was outdone by his father-in-law. Laban took advantage of Jacob again and again. But as the British poet John Dryden (1631–1700) put it, "Beware the fury of a patient man." Jacob finally exploded. But owing to a dream that set Jacob free to leave Laban (see Genesis 31:3), he took off suddenly. When Laban caught up with him, Jacob said this to him: "I worked for you for fourteen years for your two daughters and six years for your flocks, and you changed my wages ten times. . . . But God has seen my hardship and the toils of my hands, and last night he rebuked you" (Genesis 31:41–42).

Leah and Rachel

Both Leah and Rachel each had her own ambition. Leah could have children but never won the love of her husband, Jacob. Rachel was barren while Jacob was devoted to her. Rachel's heart's desire was to have children. Leah lived for one thing: to win her husband. Leah hoped that producing children would turn Jacob around. It did not. With each child Leah hoped that her husband would love her. She eventually gave up and pursued a different ambition: to praise the Lord (see Genesis 29:35). Leah the un-loved woman came to terms with the holiest pursuit of all—to focus on God. The irony is, Jacob never appreciated Leah, and yet Leah's children arguably did the most for the Kingdom of

God. Her children included Levi, the tribe that produced Moses and the Levitical Law, and Judah, through whom Messiah came.

Can Ambition Be Taught?

I am sure there are exceptions, but generally speaking, you cannot teach a person to be ambitious after he or she has grown up. He or she either has it or not. And almost certainly such ambition is the consequence of the way we were brought up. It may have come from driven parents. Sometimes it originates in sibling rivalry. It may arise from having a role model who instills a goal in one's heart. It may come from a childhood trauma that makes a person want to overcome hardships. It may have come from being extremely poor—out of which came a resolve to make money.

But can a person have too much ambition? Yes. It is what leads to unrealistic goals, paves the way for being an uncaring manipulator of people and also fertilizes the soil for being a bad parent—as King David was. Jacob and David—two of the most prominent men in the Old Testament—were probably the worst parents in ancient Israelite history. They were also among the most driven men in Israelite history.

Unambitious people often do not understand—or appreciate—those who are ambitious. Sometimes ambitiousness is resented by those who, simply, are not ambitious. Ambitious people frequently look down on those who are not strongly motivated, and unmotivated people are often unappreciative of the Donald Trumps or the Steve Jobs of this world. Dr. Clyde Narramore said, "All behavior is caused." He is best known for saying, "Every person is worth understanding." This should caution those of us who are quick to point the finger at other persons who may seem unpleasant if not obnoxious. If we knew how they were brought up and became knowledgeable of their deprivations or privileges and could somehow get into their skin, we might lower our voices and be forgiving.

What is a person to do who has too much ambition? Admit it. Pour your heart out to God and ask for mercy in order to find grace to help (see Hebrews 4:16). As for my own failure to be a good parent as the children were growing up, God has graciously been restoring "the years the locusts have eaten" (Joel 2:25). I am also trying hard to apply Paul's words that we are "not our own"—that we are "bought with a price," being "temples of the Holy Spirit." Although the context of 1 Corinthians 6:19–20 refers to misuse of the body owing to sexual promiscuity, it is certainly fair to say that we should look after the health of our own bodies. I pray every day to know when to say no and yes to invitations—whether to write books or accept a preaching engagement.

We saw earlier in this book that some of the gold medalists in the Olympics were driven by not being able to cope with losing. And yet Chris Evert, one of the all-time favorite tennis players (she won three singles championships at Wimbledon and eighteen Grand Slams), said her father taught her not to be afraid to lose. I think we all can learn from this example, especially if God allows some of us to preach a bad sermon (horrible feeling) or write a book that fails to be a good seller (which can be good for a huge ego).

Seven Principles

For those of us who may feel we have too much motivation or ambition, I offer the following suggestions:

1. Do not see your ambition as a virtue or vice but accept yourself as being the way God has made you.

2. Do not feel self-righteous about being highly motivated, as if you are a cut above others.

3. Do not look down on those who are less motivated than you or who do not have goals for their lives.

4. Remember that your body is the temple of the Holy Spirit; do not over work, get overtired or take on responsibility that will cause you to lose sleep or peace.

5. Do not neglect your family, your loved ones and those who need you and your time.

6. When you find yourself becoming irritable and hard to get along with, consider that you have stretched yourself beyond what God has required of you.

7. Resolve that your motivation and goals will be carried out entirely and solely for the glory of God.

Too Much Spiritual Ambition?

Can a person have too much ambition at the spiritual level? Yes. You may be surprised that I say this. You can be overly conscientious and try too hard to excel by trying to impress God with your diligence. The worst thing is that you can become self-righteous about being ambitious, thinking you are better than others who are not so motivated. I have been guilty of this. But it is so silly to try to impress God and "show Him" how much you want to please Him. He sees right through all of us. He knows our frame and remembers that we are dust (see Psalm 103:14). Any desire we have to please God was given by Him in the first place. "A man can receive only what is given him from heaven" (John 3:27). I will make some further recommendations in the final chapter.

I close this section of the book by urging all of us not to take ourselves too seriously. Too much ambition is counterproductive. It will make you physically ill. Too much honey will make you vomit. The consequence of too much ambition will also make us repulsive to others—the last thing that we want in our efforts to please the Lord.

Slow down. Calm down. Relax. Jesus' yoke is easy and His burden is light (see Matthew 11:30). When your burden has become too heavy—whether it be from natural or spiritual ambition—you have put yourself under a strain that God did not put there. This means you are stepping out on your own, leaving God behind—not unlike Joseph and Mary carrying on when they thought Jesus was with them but was not (see Luke 2:44).

God does not promote us to the level of our incompetence; neither does He lead us to try to do what we are unable to do.

Ambition and Money

Whoever loves money never has money enough; whoever loves wealth is never satisfied with his income. This too is meaningless.

Ecclesiastes 5:10

"No one can serve two masters. Either he will hate the one and love the other, or he will be devoted to the one and despise the other. You cannot serve both God and Money. . . . But seek first [God's] kingdom and his righteousness, and all these things will be given to you as well."

Matthew 6:24, 33

People who want to get rich fall into temptation and a trap and into many foolish and harmful desires that plunge men into ruin and destruction. For the love of money is a root of all kinds of evil. Some people, eager for money, have wandered from the faith and pierced themselves with many griefs.

1 Timothy 6:9–10

Success is a lousy teacher. It seduces smart men into thinking they can't lose.

Bill Gates (b. 1955)

When a fellow says, "It ain't the money but the principle of the thing," it's the money.

Frank M. Hubbard (1868–1930)

Although I have been a highly ambitious man all my life, for some reason I have never been particularly ambitious to be rich. This may be because I knew that being in the ministry would not ever make me rich—so thinking along the lines of being wealthy never crossed my mind. If so, perhaps I am not very qualified to write this chapter. But I do so because of what I know about the warnings and promises in the Bible and what I have observed from personal experience and observations.

My first church in Palmer, Tennessee, paid me a weekly salary of $37.50, not bad for a student pastor (in those days). But it was not quite enough to cover all my expenses at the time. Although I have learned since it is an old cliché, my church treasurer said to me almost every week, "God will keep you humble and we will keep you poor."

Two things shaped my thinking and attitude toward money fairly early on in my ministry: (1) the trauma of being in debt; and (2) a vow (rightly or wrongly) not to try to make money outside what my ministry directly paid me. The first refers to the exorbitant debt I got into before I married Louise. Among other things I had bought a new 1957 Edsel, a Cessna 120 airplane and other foolish expenditures that prohibited my going into full-time ministry for a good while. During this time I worked as a door-to-door vacuum cleaner salesman to get out of debt. The trauma of debt left such an indelible impression on me that we have not been in debt—not even a penny—for more than fifty years. I still have awful dreams—sometimes several a month—that I am still selling vacuum cleaners back in South Florida. But at least one good thing came from this hard era: I learned how to handle money.

Possibly the greatest football coach in American history was Vince Lombardi. When asked what was the secret to his success—winning more games than any coach before him—he replied: "Winning isn't the main thing, it is the only thing." I would say that about the *anointing*: It is not the main thing, it is the only thing. Billy Graham once said that his greatest fear was that God would take His hand off him. It is my greatest fear, too. There is, however, more than one way we can forfeit the anointing. But it is usually from one of the following: money, sex and power.

A Reminder of Our Inheritance

Early in this book I introduced the concept of inheritance. Every Christian is called to come into his or her inheritance. Once saved, always saved; but salvation does not automatically mean that one will persist in faith in order to come into one's inheritance and achieve a reward at the Judgment Seat of Christ. When Jesus spoke of how hard it is for a rich man to enter the Kingdom of God, He was not so much referring to a person initially coming to Christ in faith but coming into his inheritance after being saved (see Mark 10:25). We are saved by transferring our trust in good works to what Jesus Christ did for us by His death on the cross. Salvation is not by works but by sheer grace (see Ephesians 2:8–9). The one who believes from the heart that Jesus died on the cross and was raised from the dead is eternally saved. But to *inherit* the Kingdom comes from our attitude and behavior—and largely regarding money, sex and power.

> But among you there must not be even a hint of sexual immorality, or of any kind of impurity, or of greed, because these are improper for God's holy people. Nor should there be obscenity, foolish talk or coarse joking, which are out of place, but rather thanksgiving. For of this you can be sure: No immoral, impure or greedy person—such a man is an idolater—has any inheritance in the kingdom of Christ and of God. Let no one deceive you with empty words, for because of such things God's wrath comes on those who are disobedient. Therefore do not be partners with them.
>
> Ephesians 5:3–7

Christians who give in to greed—like Ananias and Sapphira—because they *are* saved will be the object of the wrath of God in the present life. If they were not truly saved, God would have let them alone and let them be condemned later with the world. The wrath of God in this case, then, is not a reference to eternal punishment but the severe chastening of the Lord in the here and now. It comes upon those Christians who were not persisting in faith and obedience.

How God's Wrath Is Manifested

The wrath of God in this life is manifested in at least four ways.

First, the immediate, *premature or sudden death of believers*, like that of Ananias and Sapphira (see Acts 5:1–10). This kind of judgment was referred to by Paul when he warned those in Corinth who had abused the Lord's Supper. In those days they did not have church buildings as we have today but worshiped in homes, usually large homes owned by wealthier people. Certain Christians who were financially and socially better off—what we might call middle or even upper class—showed contempt for the poor by administering Holy Communion without them (because the working class had to work late and did not arrive on time). In not waiting for the poorer Christians to arrive, these richer people drank "judgment" on themselves. The lower-class Christians were isolated and marginalized. They possibly thought nobody cared. They may have thought that even God did not notice what was going on. But God noticed. These wealthier believers may have thought what they did—partaking of Holy Communion before the lower-class Christians arrived—was minor. But it stirred the heart of God. This, says Paul, is precisely why some had "fallen asleep"—a euphemism that refers to Christians who have died (1 Corinthians 11:30). John calls it "a sin that leads to death" (1 John 5:16).

I must pause at this stage and say something further about well-to-do Christians and the poor. Christianity today, certainly in the West, is largely middle class. There is smugness in middle-class Christians that is displeasing to God. There is sometimes a haughty attitude in some Christians when they think of the poor or unemployed: "Let them find a job—they are lazy, just wanting handouts." We who are middle class do not realize how this grieves the Holy Spirit. We dismiss the poor as we carry on with our middle-class values without the slightest tinge of conscience. This arrogant spirit is in many of us unconsciously, and we do not begin to grasp how this is wrong in the sight of God. Since there is no thunder, no lightning and no sudden sign of God's displeasure, we do not give our neglect of the poor the slightest thought.

But God notices. God loves the poor. God has chosen the poor of this world to be rich in faith (see James 2:5). By the way, the book of James is now said to be the favorite New Testament book in the Third World. I do not want to be among those who say to the Lord at the Judgment, "'When did we see *you* hungry or thirsty or a stranger or needing clothes or sick or in prison, and did not help you?' [Then Jesus] will reply, 'I tell you the truth, whatever you did not do for one of the least of these, you did not do for me'" (Matthew 25:44–45, emphasis added). If we middle-class Christians do not get a wake-up call *now*, it will mean an awakening on that Last Day when it is too late. Our attitude and response to the poor does not determine whether we go to heaven or hell, but it certainly pertains to our inheritance here below and our reward (or absence of it) at the Judgment Seat of Christ.

James said, "You have insulted the poor" (James 2:6; Gr. *ptochon*—accusative, masculine, singular, which means "poor man"). Indeed, the English Standard Version translates this word as "the poor man." Furthermore, this translation paves the way for the only interpretation that makes sense of James 2:14 (emphasis added): "Can faith save *him*?" (accusative, masculine, singular). *Him* refers directly to the "poor man" of James 2:6. Scholars over the centuries have assumed that James changed the subject from the poor man to assurance of salvation by the time he got to James 2:14. James is *still* talking about the same poor man throughout James 2! Once you see that James 2:14 refers to the same poor man, the rest of the chapter reads by itself—and removes the issue of whether or not a person is saved by works! James demonstrates how God cares for the poor and how Christians must not merely say "God bless you" (see verse 16) but *do something*—to impress upon the poor people of this world that we really do care. This is what will get the attention of the poor and lead many to salvation. It is why God raised up The Salvation Army. It is the reason God often starts a new movement among the poor. The problem is, when the poor become middle class (it often happens), they forget the poor, too!

In any case, the judgment upon the Christians of Corinth was owing to their treatment of the poor working-class Christians who did not get to participate in the Lord's Supper because they arrived too late. Paul tells these people that it "is not the Lord's Supper you eat" when you behave like that (1 Corinthians 11:20). Stop calling it the Lord's Supper when you treat the poor like that, Paul is saying.

Ananias and Sapphira, no doubt middle-class Christians, were struck dead by trying to be very "in" with those who truly sold their property and gave it to the apostles for distribution. Those in Corinth had premature deaths owing to their insulting the poor—the thing James warns about. Dr. Tony Campolo shocked the students at Wheaton College some years ago when he said to them, "You people don't give a s— about the poor." He then said five minutes later, "And the problem is you are thinking more about my saying 's—' than you do about the poor." Do you think Tony might have been right?

Dear reader, are you getting the message?

Second, some were *judged by being "weak and sick"*—which shows how God gets one's attention through putting us flat on our backs. In other words, some of these middle-class Christians were taken prematurely to heaven, others of them who had abused the poor were inflicted with illness or some disease. I have to tell you that some of God's best servants have succumbed to the love of money but have also known severe chastening. Never forget, however, that such chastening comes to those who are *saved*—whom the Lord "loves" (Hebrews 12:6). As we saw earlier, "When we are judged by the Lord, we are being disciplined [chastened, KJV] so that we will not be condemned with the world" (1 Corinthians 11:32).

Being condemned with the world means going to hell. Being disciplined, or chastened, means being punished in the here and now. The Greek word that is translated "chastening" or "being disciplined" essentially means *"enforced learning."* I have on occasion been forced to watch the pain and agony of friends whose business dealings were not always above board—all owing to the love of money. I have been called to the bedside of wealthy people who were in terrible pain and suffering—asking me to pray that they be healed or spared. I would, of course, do my best to pray for them, but in my heart of hearts I felt some of these people were being chastened by the Lord owing to their mishandling of money. Some people respond positively to such chastening. God's wrath brings one to see that such love for money "wasn't worth it." Indeed, the love of money is a root of all kinds of evil. "People *who want to get rich* fall into temptation and a trap and into many foolish and harmful desires that plunge men into ruin and destruction" (1 Timothy 6:9, emphasis added).

Was Paul being too strong here? Are there not exceptions? Does not God give to some an unusual ability to create wealth for His glory? I believe so, as I will repeat in more detail below. Some of the godliest people I have known are wealthy. I do not think, however, that many are called to be like that. I think Paul was speaking along the lines of a general principle to warn all of us against greed.

Do you want to get rich? Do you have a love of money? Be warned. You could be a ripe candidate for "temptation" and a "trap," vulnerable to "foolish and harmful desires." If you are not careful you could come to ruin and destruction. God is no respecter of persons. He loves poor people. He gave you a good income, but how do you use this money? Are you a tither? Do you care about the poor? Are you honest in your business dealings? Would you be happy for God's spotlight to be on your income and use of money for everybody to see? By the way, at the Judgment there will be nothing "hidden" or "kept secret." It will all be out in the open.

If, however, you are not beset with a desire to be rich, you should thank God for this. Be very thankful. You have no idea how blessed you are. Whatever you do, do not feel sorry for yourself because you are not driving a Mercedes-Benz or Rolls-Royce (see Psalm 37:1). Those people who have lots of money can be among the most pitiful, tragic and impoverished people in the world. When I sold vacuum cleaners I met many rich people. I sold to the founder of Pepsi-Cola, to the heiress of Coca-Cola, to the owner of the Empire State Building, to the president of Ford Motor Company. I could go on and on. Never in my life have I seen such pathetic people. What about those who are believers but persist not in obedience but in shady dealings and dishonesty when it comes to money? If they are not brought to premature death or sickness, there follows yet another option.

Third, some are *judged by becoming "stone deaf"* to the voice of the Holy Spirit. The writer of Hebrews cautioned that his readers had become hard of hearing, that is, they were decreasingly able to hear God speak (see Hebrews 5:11 KJV, ESV). The worst scenario—that they would be inflicted with stone deafness—is God's anger on His own people. Deafness at the natural level often comes in stages. First, you cup your hand over your ear when people speak. Second, you get a hearing aid. Third, a stronger hearing aid. The worst state: You are profoundly deaf, stone deaf; you cannot hear a thing.

Stone deafness sadly happens at the spiritual level to some Christians in this life. It may not necessarily be because of their attitude to the poor. This is possible, but stone deafness comes to those who, after repeated warnings, cross over a line and reach the point of no return in their spiritual lives. The consequence in the case of certain Hebrew Christians was that they could not be renewed again to repentance (Hebrew 6:4–6).

Perhaps you know that Hebrews 6:4–6 has been a theological battleground among Christians for centuries. Those who say (like some Calvinists) you cannot "fall away" do not like this passage; it clearly talks about those who "fall away" (the Greek, in fact, is literally translated "having fallen away"—it already happened with some). But those who (like some Arminians) teach that you can fall away do not like this passage because they teach that you *can* be restored, but it says if you do fall away you cannot come back!

What does this passage mean? The key is Hebrews 5:11, where the writer picks up the subject (raised in Hebrews 3:15) of hearing God speak. The reference to dullness of hearing is the key to Hebrews 6:4–6. *These were saved people who will be in heaven.* They not only had been granted repentance—which shows they had been truly converted—but reached the place they could not be renewed "again" (Gr. *palin*) to repentance. Stone deafness means you cannot hear. Stone deafness to the Holy Spirit means you cannot hear God speak anymore. They were once given repentance. They also knew what it was to be renewed. But no more, says the writer; they could not be renewed "again." They finally crossed over a line. Repentance is always something that is "granted"; it is what God graciously bestows or leads one to (Romans 2:4).

Be thankful for any repentance you have; it is a gift of God. But if you are unable to be renewed you are like King Saul, who had become unteachable and unreachable. Do not let it happen to you. This means that no longer would such people be changed from "glory to glory" (2 Corinthians 3:18) but would live the rest of their lives without an ability to repent or hear God speak to their hearts. It is a horrible judgment. I fear that I have witnessed this very thing in some people in my 57 years of ministry. Greed, however, is not the only thing that brings about this kind of judgment. But it often is. We must all be very careful when it comes to money and the love of money. John refers "boasting of what [one] has and does" (1 John 2:16; the "pride of life," KJV). It is so easy to feel good about your prestigious job, your fine home, beautiful clothes, your car, your connections. It is easy to rationalize expenses and cut corners—thinking nobody will find out. But God knows. We all need to be extremely cautious. The key: keeping a warm, honest and docile heart that enables us to hear God speak. As long as we can hear His voice, good. But let us all be wary. This is why the admonition "Today, if you hear his voice" (Hebrews 3:7) precedes this scary section of Hebrews.

Fourth, all will be *exposed at the Judgment Seat of Christ.* We must all stand before Jesus Christ one day—every single one of us—and give an account of the deeds done in the body (see 2 Corinthians 5:10). Nothing will be hidden then. Be sure of that. Why does God tell us in advance about the Judgment Seat of Christ? Mainly so we may anticipate and avoid unspeakable pain on that occasion. All motives will be exposed. All shady dealings revealed. Those who have been conscientious, who have walked in the light and have kept two-way communication with the Holy Spirit, will receive a reward on that day. Paul calls it building a superstructure over the foundation of gold, silver, precious stones. The reward at the Judgment Seat of Christ will be based upon our superstructure. Gold, silver, precious stones cannot be burned by fire. But those who build a superstructure of wood, hay, straw will be saved but by fire. The wood, hay and straw will be burned up—gone. Those who have not persisted in faith and obedience will be "saved" but by fire (1 Corinthians 3:15).

The worst destiny of all, however, is, of course, eternal punishment. This will be meted out to the lost. Paul's reference to being condemned with the world (see 1 Corinthians 11:32) means eternal punishment to those not saved. Being saved from the "coming wrath" (1 Thessalonians 1:10) is a reference to eternal punishment. There are only two destinies for all humankind after death: heaven or hell. I am sorry, but that is it. So I must ask you once more: Do you know for sure that if you were to die today you would go to heaven? I also ask: If you were to stand before God (and you will) and He were to ask you (and He might), "Why should I let you into My heaven?" what would you say? If you are trusting in your good works, your prosperity, your church attendance, baptism, being brought up in a Christian home or feel you have done enough good works to merit heaven, I must lovingly tell you: You are as lost as anybody could be. I do you no favor not to tell you that. But if you were to pray this prayer, you can know you are saved—that is, if you mean this and say it from your heart:

> *Lord Jesus Christ, I need You. I want You. I am sorry for my sins. I know I cannot save myself. I know my good*

works will not save me. I trust Your death on the cross. Wash my sins away by Your blood. I welcome Your Holy Spirit into my heart. As best as I know how, I give You my life. Amen.

If that prayer is from your heart, you must show how much you really mean this by: (1) reading your Bible every day, (2) praying daily—developing a consistent prayer life, (3) being a part of a church where the Bible is preached and Jesus Christ is honored, (4) witnessing for Christ daily; do not be ashamed of your praying this prayer.

The truth is, those who have prayed this prayer but do not persist in faith (see Colossians 2:6–7) will fall into the exact same category I have been writing about in this book. The worst thing that can happen to any person is to be eternally lost. But next to that would be to be exposed and dealt with at the Judgment Seat of Christ. I again have a word for those who say, "I don't care about a reward at the Judgment Seat of Christ; I just want to know I will go to heaven": *You won't think that way then!* This is why a reward, or the "prize," was so important to Paul and why he disciplined himself so that, having preached to others, he would not be rejected for that prize (1 Corinthians 9:27).

My father named me after his favorite minister, Dr. R. T. Williams. Dad used to tell me that Dr. Williams, after ordaining people to the ministry, would say: "Young men, beware of two things in your ministry: money and women. If there is a scandal connected with either, God will forgive you but the people won't."

My father was neither a brilliant nor rich man but the godliest man I have known. He meant well in driving me to excel. My first memory of my dad was seeing him on his knees daily for some thirty minutes before he went to work. He was not a minister; he was a layman—a rate clerk for the Chesapeake and Ohio Railway Company. He was also a consistent tither all his life. As I said in my book *Tithing*, my father taught me to tithe. Louise and I have been consistent tithers for more than fifty years. Having made huge mistakes when it came to money early in my ministry, I have been attracted to that verse, "It is good for a man to bear the yoke while he is young" (Lamentations 3:27). I was chastened and taught well.

I have also learned from the folly of others. I have watched what the love of money has done to some of my friends. I saw how a desire to get rich broke up marriages. One of my earliest memories was hearing a friend's comment, "But it's money in my pocket," when he justified a decision that steered him away from godly principles. He went into the world. "It's money in my pocket" seemed to make it right for him. It certainly does *not* make it right, and any person reading these lines should be scared nearly to death at the thought of being deceitful and nefarious when it comes to money matters.

Tithing

The only time in my life I asked a publisher to publish a book for me was when I wanted to write a book on tithing. The publisher eventually said yes on the condition I would purchase one thousand copies. Agreed. They obviously did not think it would sell. That book is still in print more than thirty years later—on both sides of the Atlantic. It is a needed book—more than ever. It has been endorsed by Billy Graham, John Stott, Sir Fred Catherwood and Lord Carey, former Archbishop of Canterbury.

Many ministers are loathe to preach on tithing lest their congregations suspect their motives. This should not bother them. It is utterly and totally scriptural. In any case, here I am retired with no church (except the one we attend—and give our tithe to), so I do not see how anyone could suspect my motive in bringing up this unpopular subject. Please read my book *Tithing*, but here are the headlines:

1. *The tithe is the Lord's* (see Leviticus 27:30). Abraham believed that the tithe belonged to God four hundred years before Moses made it legal. It means that one-tenth of our earnings is *already* God's; He puts us on our honor to give it back to Him. Those who do not—or pay less than the tithe—are said to be robbing God (see Malachi 3:8). In other words, if you earn $10,000 and give nothing, you have robbed God of $1,000. If you earn $10,000 and give $200 to the church, you have robbed Him of $980.

2. *God promised to bless those who tithe, even when they were under the Law.* What fascinates me about this is that God did not have to promise blessing at that stage; they were required by Law to do it. But He lovingly and tenderly speaks to our interest by motivating us to give Him what is His. "See if I will not throw open the floodgates of heaven and pour out so much blessing that you will not have room enough for it" (Malachi 3:10). It was true then, it is true now.

3. *Jesus' death on the cross puts us back to the pre-Mosaic Law era.* The Law (a 1,300-year parenthesis—from 1300 BC to AD 33) was fulfilled when Jesus died, and puts us in the very position of Abraham, the first tither. We are *not* under the Law; we are *not* required to tithe as a prerequisite to salvation. We do it out of gratitude; after all, it is God's prescribed method of supporting the Gospel. Some do,

some do not. Those who do are blessed; those who do not are impoverished (whether they know it or not).

4. *Jesus endorsed tithing* (see Matthew 23:23). In Matthew 23 when Jesus refuted and lambasted the Pharisees point by point, He gave them their dues on one issue: They tithed! It is the *only* thing they did that He agreed with! This is weighty. Jesus was a tither (see Matthew 5:17). As we follow Him by being baptized, as we also follow Him to be more like Him, let us follow His example in being a tither.

5. *It is a part of persistent faith by which we come into our inheritance.* Tithing does not save us—it does not even help toward our salvation. Salvation is *free*—by faith alone in Christ alone. But as every Christian is called to come into his or her inheritance, part of that calling is fulfilled by our being generous givers. Tithing is only the beginning. But be sure you begin with the one-tenth!

Matthew 6:33

My father's favorite verse—he must have quoted it to me a thousand times—was: "Seek ye first the kingdom of God, and his righteousness; and all these shall be added unto you" (Matthew 6:33 KJV). What are "all these things"? Answer: the essential needs of life—food, shelter and clothing. In the middle of the Sermon on the Mount Jesus explains that it is our heavenly Father's promise to look after all of us and all of our *needs*.

> "Do not worry about your life, what you will eat or drink; or about your body, what you will wear. Is not life more important than food, and the body more important than clothes? . . . So do not worry, saying, 'What shall we eat?' or 'What shall we drink?' or 'What shall we wear?' For the pagans run after all these things, and your heavenly Father knows that you need

them. But seek first his kingdom and his righteousness, and all these things will be given to you as well."

Matthew 6:25, 31–33

Are Some Christians Called to Be Rich?

Yes. I grant that some people can handle a lot of money. There are some Christians who can be trusted with wealth. I accept, too, that some are *called* to earn a lot of money, make money, earn huge salaries and glorify God by doing so. I have known some of these people. I am a mentor to some of them, and I can testify that some of the wealthiest people I have known are among the godliest I have ever met. I doubt, however, that there are many who are called to be wealthy and who can be trusted with a lot of money. I think they are very few indeed. What a pity then that some ministers—especially on TV—entice innocent Christians with the notion that God wants them to be rich! I would not want to be in the shoes of such preachers who make these claims.

One caution to the wealthy: Unless you are unique, you probably do not tithe. You probably imagine that your thousands are of more value than the few dollars or pounds that the lower income people give. Wrong. Very, very wrong. God values the poor man's tithe, the poor woman's tithe as much as your tithe (see Luke 21:1–3). And if you give *less* than the tithe, you have robbed God. When I was pastor of the Lauderdale Manors Baptist Church in Fort Lauderdale, I happened to find out one Monday morning who gave and who did not. In some ways I wish the treasurer had never shared this with me. To my astonishment, the most consistent givers were not the high income people, but the widows, the divorcees and those on low incomes.

I am sorry, but this is typical. *Shame on you*—non-tithing physician, lawyer, banker, stock broker, dentist, computer expert! Shame, shame, shame on you. Your love of money will sooner or later impoverish you. By the way, there will be no tithing in heaven. Give God what is His while you can.

Suggestions to Those Who Struggle with Money

Are you a person who struggles with money, finances and a love of money? I now offer these principles:

1. *Do not feel guilty about this.* You are not alone. We all struggle with these issues. This is why Jesus devoted a big chunk of His Sermon on the Mount to money and worry over finances (see Matthew 6:19–34).

2. *Remember that God assumes responsibility to supply our needs* (see Philippians 4:19). Remind God of His own promise to supply your need when you fear you will not have enough. The best and most effective kind of praying is to remind God of His own Word!

3. *Avoid debt if you possibly can, and do not use a credit card to charge for things you cannot pay for in full when it is due.* In the Lord's Prayer we pray, "Give us this day our daily bread" (Matthew 6:11 KJV), which refers to all our essential needs—one day at a time.

4. *Do not justify greed or the eagerness to get rich.* This is "wisdom" that comes not from heaven but from below. Fight "love of money" as you would sexual temptation; refuse to give in to it.

5. *Give God the tithe that He claims for Himself.* Abraham was the first tither; he is the proto-Christian. I remind you

that the Gospel puts us in Abraham's position as if there were no Law (see Galatians 3:6–20). What is more, you cannot out-give the Lord.

6. *Live within your income.* Live on the 90 percent you get to keep for yourself. You will spare yourself agony down the road.

7. *Be thankful for what you have.* God loves gratitude; He hates ingratitude. Psychologists have shown that thankful people live longer!

When I was pastor of a small church in Carlisle, Ohio, my doctrine so displeased a number of the people that they got up a petition to run us off. They eventually succeeded. In the meantime, the people withheld their giving—to starve us. It almost worked. The treasurer had to cut my small salary into one-half. We barely had money for food and gasoline, but we never stopped tithing. I will never forget one day when Louise and I had no money in the bank and we did not know how we would make it that day. But in the mail that very day a check for $25 came from a couple we had not seen in years. I did not even know they knew how to reach us. But they did. A woman several hundred miles away awoke one morning and said to her husband, "We need to send R. T. and Louise $25." That money was pure gold to us. Do not tell me that God does not look after His own!

When we are having hard times it is easy to look for a way out in order to avoid our financial responsibility to God and His Church. I have had people send me articles against tithing. Some say they are not against giving but do not believe in the principle of tithing since "all our money belongs to God." It is a neat way to avoid tithing. But, remember, as we say in Kentucky, quoting from a well-known cartoonist of a previous generation, "When a fellow says, 'It ain't the money but the principle of the thing,' it's the money."

All our money does indeed belong to God. We must be ambitious to please Him when it comes to how we handle it. God does not promise us luxury. He promises to take care of us—what we need. We can have luxury in heaven. It is worth waiting for.

Finishing Well

I consider my life worth nothing to me, if only I may finish the race and complete the task the Lord Jesus has given me—the task of testifying to the gospel of God's grace.

Acts 20:24

I have fought the good fight, I have finished the race, I have kept the faith. Now there is in store for me the crown of righteousness, which the Lord, the righteous Judge, will award to me on that day—and not only to me, but also to all who have longed for his appearing.

2 Timothy 4:7–8

Pray for me, that I will finish well.

John Stott (1921–2011)
to Lyndon Bowring
a few weeks before he died

It ain't over till it's over.

Yogi Berra (b. 1925)

My research at Oxford focused largely on the English Puritans. They had been my heroes for many years. But when I began to study their theology in close detail, I became somewhat disillusioned with many of them. What was disappointing for me was to discover how few of them died with any assurance of their own salvation. Incredible. But this was largely because they based their assurance of going to heaven on their sanctification rather than trusting Christ alone. They thought they trusted Christ for their salvation, yes; but the *assurance* that they were really trusting Christ was grounded in their own godliness. They often reminded me of the very legalism I had been set free from in my earlier years. As Dr. J. I. Packer put it, they sought godliness more than God. When we do it that way, there will always be a doubt whether we are "in" or "out." After all, our hearts are deceitful above all things and "beyond cure" (Jeremiah 17:9).

The thesis of this book is that we should channel our ambition into one direction: seeking the glory of God and, with that, if possible, getting all of Him we possibly can. We can do this as King David did, who narrowed all his desires down to *one*: to behold the beauty of the Lord and to dwell in His presence (see Psalm 27:4). Never forget, however, that seeking after God in this way is not trying to get ourselves saved. We seek after God in this manner because we have been saved. Salvation is God's free gift. If we accept this gift on the basis of being sorry for our sins and confessing them to God because Jesus Christ paid our debt by His precious blood, we are saved. This way we put the issue of whether or not we are saved behind us and press on to receive the inheritance to which every Christian is called.

Being ambitious to glorify God is the way we receive our inheritance. As we persist in faith—in the same faith that justified us (see Colossians 2:6–7), we will surely come into our inheritance. Remember that this inheritance is primarily *internal*—intimacy with God—and secondarily *external*, discovering God's plan for our lives. Do not try to figure out what God's plan for your life is first; this will take care of itself as you keep your eyes on Jesus (see Hebrews 12:2).

Integrity

I referred above to Jeremiah 17:9, that our hearts are deceitful and incurably wicked. We see this about ourselves as we move closer to the throne of God. When Isaiah saw the glory of the Lord he cried out, "Woe to me! I am ruined!" (see Isaiah 6:5). For years I had assumed that certain "godly" desires I have had were truly God-honoring. Perhaps. But I am not so sure now. I have said, for example, that I want a "double anointing" of the Holy Spirit. And I really do. But could this be a fleshly wish as well as spiritual? Yes.

Some years ago we were invited to visit certain churches in the old Soviet Union. My translator, Sergei Nikolaev, said to me one evening, "R. T., what do you want God to do most in all the world?" I replied, "Revival in Westminster Chapel." He asked, "Why?" I thought it was a rather foolish question. "Why wouldn't I?" I replied. "It would be wonderful." But he countered, "What if revival came to a different church in London, would you be happy then?" He got me! But his word had such an impact on me that I began not only to pray for other churches in London but publicly stated: "If revival came to All Souls or Kensington Temple, would we affirm it?"

Mind you, I never thought I would have to do that. I was certain that if revival came to London it would be to Westminster

Chapel! But one day I had to prove whether or not I really meant what I had been preaching. A surprising move of the Holy Spirit came suddenly to Holy Trinity Brompton—right in the heart of Knightsbridge, London. When I heard what was going on I was offended. I did not like what I heard (people falling to the floor and laughing their heads off after being prayed for). For one thing, if it really and truly was of God, it would have surely come to Westminster Chapel first! How could God do this? I almost felt betrayed by God. How dare God bypass us who had prayed so hard for the manifestation of the glory of God in our midst!

That movement of the Spirit was called the Toronto Blessing—the place of its origin. I first spoke publicly against it, saying, "We do need to be open to whatever God may choose to do, but this is not *it*." I came later to see that it was indeed a work of God. Indeed, I began to fear that I myself might be in the tradition of those who were against historic moves of the Holy Spirit—for example, the Great Awakening (1735–1750) and the Welsh Revival (1904–1905). There were "sound" people who were against these movements of God, all of them stating their seemingly plausible reasons. The Great Awakening was criticized for strange manifestations among other things. The Welsh Revival was criticized for lack of preaching. When we are unhappy with something it is not hard to come up with theological reasons that appear to justify our positions. In the matter of what was going on at Holy Trinity Brompton, I later went to our pulpit and climbed down, stating that a work of God was happening at HTB and encouraging people to go there. And some did.

My point is this. When we speak of the glory of God, it means that the *God of glory*—not us or our distinctive doctrinal point of view—will be honored and glorified. When we get to heaven *His* honor and praise will be the only thing that matters. There will be no rival spirit in heaven. No threatened egos. And no ambition. That absence of a rival spirit is precisely what needs to be brought forward to the here and now *now*—to be ambitious for *God* to be glorified rather than seeing ourselves vindicated.

One way, therefore, we must be ambitious for God is to let Him off the hook if He chooses to *withhold* His blessing from us. We honor Him truly when we affirm Him for what He *does not* do as well as what He does.

Is This All There Is?

I have always been a bit of a hero worshiper. In sports it was Joe DiMaggio, in politics it would be Nelson Mandela and Winston Churchill, in Church history it would be Martin Luther and John Calvin, in biblical history it would be Moses and Paul. These are the truly great men of all time. I have always aspired to be great. Do forgive me if this candid admission offends you. James Barrie (1860–1937), the creator of Peter Pan, said that ambition is the "last infirmity of noble minds." There is a line in Shakespeare's play *Julius Caesar*: "As he was valiant, I honor him. But as he was ambitious, I slew him." But to refer to Josif Tson's observation again, Jesus never condemned James and John for aspiring to be great but rather the way one achieves greatness.

Do you know what it is to see the years pass by and wonder what you have been missing? Some call it the "midlife crisis," a feeling that life has passed you by. You ask: *Is this all there is?* Will I ever have significance, or even a touch of greatness? Jesus said that they who exalt themselves will be humbled, and they who humble themselves will be exalted (see Matthew 23:12).

Only God can make a child of God great. We have seen that it is God who chooses our inheritance for us (see Psalm 47:4). This means we can never outdo or improve on what God has predestined. At the natural level He chose our parents, the date and place of our birth, our intelligence and intellect, and how we are motivated. Not only that, He is the One who called and justified us, filled us with the Holy Spirit and determined our gift and role in the Body of Christ. In a word: What we can aspire to is actually out of our hands. God decides.

Question: Can you live with that? God could have made you a Shakespeare or a Churchill. But He didn't. He could have made me another Jonathan Edwards or Martyn Lloyd-Jones. But He didn't. He could have made you another Nelson Mandela or Albert Einstein. But He didn't. He could have made you a billionaire. But He didn't. How does this make you feel?

I answer: It brings great relief. Peace. Freedom. I am set free to the degree that I come to terms with (1) the limits of my gifting and (2) the insignificance of my place in history. This helps me to relax, slow down and say, "Thank You, Lord, that You made me and saved me, and that You don't ask me to accomplish what You never called me to achieve in the first place." It is a crime against God's sovereignty and integrity if I try to excel where God did not call me to excel or to prove what God did not require me to prove or to accomplish what was never achievable in the first place because only God could make that happen. I asked the late Carl F. H. Henry (1913–2003) what he would do differently if he had his life to live over. He was pensive. Then he replied: "I would remember that only God can change the water into wine."

Coming to terms regarding the limits of our anointing must also be paralleled by our coming to terms with what God does with *others* instead of us. You may recall that Peter wanted to know what God's will was with John (see John 21:21). Don't ask, "Why can't I have so-and-so's gifting, money, career, personality, success or ministry?" Don't ask, "Why can't I have Noah's anointing—or have favor as Enoch had?" Ask instead, "What is God sovereignly pleased to do with me?" And then embrace it with both hands. God said to Moses, "I will have mercy on whom I will have mercy, and I will have compassion on whom I will have compassion" (Exodus 33:19). This a pretty strong hint that we will never succeed in twisting God's arm to do what we may personally want. He is glorified when we are jealous for His pleasure.

Make it your ambition, then, to excel in your love for His glory. Jonathan Edwards said that the one thing that Satan cannot produce is a love for the glory of God. The devil can counterfeit many things. But not that. He hates God and His glory. He is incapable of producing in you and me a love for the glory of God. If, therefore, you have unfeigned love for the praise, honor and glory of God, you may be sure that it is an affection that did not come from the flesh or the devil. Only God can do that. I say, therefore: Be ambitious for the glory of God.

But there is more. Our reward at the Judgment Seat of Christ will be based upon our faithfulness and obedience to what God *calls* us to do, not what we achieve in our own strength. What we do by our own efforts is fleshly. It is of no value. The flesh profits or counts for "nothing" (John 6:63). It is the greatest folly to try to do what we are not called to do. There is absolutely nothing you and I can ever—ever—do in the flesh that will please God.

An unforgettable example of this is when the children of Israel decided to conquer Canaan when it was too late for them. They had their chance—and blew it. Caleb and Joshua had pleaded with the Israelites to go for it—"We can take Canaan because God is with us," they said in so many words. But Caleb and Joshua were outnumbered and the majority ruled. God then swore in His wrath that Israel would most certainly *not* enter His rest. But certain men said the next day, "We can do it." Wrong. "Don't try," said Moses. "You are fools to try," he said to them; "it has already been decided that it is too late for that." They tried anyway. And totally and utterly failed (see Numbers 14:40–45).

Here is what is required of you and me: to be faithful in that which is "least" (Luke 16:10 KJV). If you wonder if you would be able to die for Jesus, especially when you read the biographies of the great martyrs of the Church, ask if you are being obedient to what has up to now been required of you. You may feel, "I could never have died for my faith as they did. I am not that strong." I have an answer for you: If you have been faithful in the little things—going not from A to Z but from A to B—I can promise that you will be faithful in the big things—the gigantic tasks that show valiant faith and heroic deaths for Jesus Christ. The martyrs and great men and women of Church history were only human. They were just like you and me. But if you and I are faithful to what God calls us to do, however insignificant and however low the profile may be, you will please God as much as the spiritual giants of history.

Take giving, for example. The widow who gave her "all" to the Temple, said Jesus, gave more than the Jews who gave many more shekels. The wealthier people give out of their bounty, but she gave all she had. That was "more" in God's sight than what others gave, even if their contributions would add up to millions (see Luke 21:1–4). So, too, with obedience to God. You are only required to obey the Word as it is unfolded to you, and one day at a time at that. As long as you are fulfilling what God has called you to do, you are pleasing the Lord. You are pleasing Him as much as the martyrs did. Huge ambition does not please God. What pleases Him is whether or not our ambition is to please Him. Make it your ambition to please Him, said Paul (2 Corinthians 5:9). "Make it your ambition to lead a quiet life, to mind your own business and to work with your hands" (1 Thessalonians 4:11). You might not have Paul's own ambition—to preach "where Christ was not known" (Romans 15:20). But who put Paul's vision there? Did Paul have such innate goodness that he came up with that because he was a better person than you? No. He had that ambition because it was given him from heaven—it came from God not from within his creative genius (see John 3:27).

Theological Ambition

I said earlier that I sometimes wonder if there ever was a purely theological controversy that was over just doctrine without a personal interest. Perhaps there were doctrinal issues that were devoid of people's ambition for their own point of view. But the quest for sound theology is too often centered on "my" interpretation of the Bible—whether it is soteriological (doctrine of salvation), ecclesiological (doctrine of the Church, including baptism) or eschatological (doctrine of "last things," e.g., the Second Coming and Final Judgment).

Is anybody exactly right and pure theologically? This, too, must come under Paul's admonition: Wait until God Himself shows who got it right and who got it wrong on certain theological details, then each will receive "his praise from God" (1 Corinthians 4:5). I am not referring to the essentials of doctrine, as the Deity of Jesus Christ, His bodily resurrection, His substitutionary death and necessity of faith in Christ to be saved from the coming wrath of God. I refer to finer points of doctrine that the best of God's people have disagreed on—especially regarding eschatology. Those who have a need to show "I got it right" and get personally and emotionally involved betray an ambition that is self-driven rather than what is motivated by the power of the Spirit for the glory of God.

So, too, with those who have prophetic gifts. There is sadly a rivalry among prophetic people. This is nothing new. Jeremiah was challenged by false prophets (see Jeremiah 28:1–17). Not that all today who claim to have a prophetic gift are to be held in suspicion. But many of them are anxious to prove how stunning and awesome their gift is and want to be seen for it, to get credit for it and to be vindicated for it. I say to such people, "Who makes you different from anyone else? What do you have that you did not receive? And if you did receive it, why do you boast as though you did not?" (1 Corinthians 4:7).

The main thing about people like Paul is that they do not count their lives "dear" (Acts 20:24 KJV); "I consider my life worth nothing to me" (Acts 20:24). That is the irony. Surprising as it may seem, historically those who are most valuable to the Kingdom do not feel that way themselves! Those who overcame by the blood of the Lamb and by the word of their testimony, and "*did not love their lives* so much as to shrink from death" (Revelation 12:11, emphasis added). Jesus said he who loves his life will lose it and he who loses it will find it (see Mark 8:35). God gives adequate grace to each of us to do this.

One of the most encouraging promises is Psalm 37:4: "Delight yourself in the LORD and he will give you the desires of your heart." But to repeat what Dr. Michael Eaton has noted, "When

God does not appear to keep His word He offers a temporary substitute, which in fact is far better." Absolutely true. No good thing does He withhold from those who walk uprightly (Psalm 84:11). If we feel deprived over what *has not* happened to us in the light of what we had hoped would happen, I guarantee this: You will not always feel this way. The whole picture is not unfolded yet. When the entire picture is revealed—even if it is delayed until we get to heaven—there will be no sorrow then. No disappointment then. No regrets then.

The approval of God should be our goal. If so, the conscious approval of God will be our reward. That would be enough.

I want to finish well. I have had people say to me (they mean well): "You are proof of someone finishing well." I want to reply, to quote Yogi Berra: "It ain't over till it's over." If I die today, yes, I believe, just maybe, I will have finished fairly well. But I could live a few more years—and still blow it big-time. Believe me, I know what I am talking about. I do not want to bring disgrace upon the name of Christ by unsanctified ambition or by any other weakness of the flesh that resides in me. It does not get easier as we get older. When you are my age you will agree. "It ain't over till it's over."

In the meantime we can take heart from these words:

A man can do nothing better than to eat and drink and find satisfaction in his work. This too, I see, is from the hand of God, for without him, who can eat or find enjoyment? To the man who pleases him, God gives wisdom, knowledge and happiness.

Ecclesiastes 2:24–26

I began this book by referring to the 2012 London Olympics. I suppose the most thrilling moments of the Olympics come when those men or women who win the gold are awarded it in front of millions. It is impossible to imagine the ecstasy they must be feeling as their own national anthems are being played in that tearful moment.

But I can think of something more thrilling than that. It will come at the Judgment Seat of Christ. It is when we hear from the lips of Jesus Himself—as He looks right into our eyes and says, "Well done. Good." Nothing can get better than that. It is a moment to be ambitious for. It is a moment worth waiting for.

I pray that this book has helped direct your ambition to want precisely that.

May God the Father, Son and Holy Spirit bless you and keep you, cause His face to shine upon you and give you peace now and evermore. Amen.

Dr. R. T. Kendall was born in Ashland, Kentucky, on July 13, 1935. He has been married to Louise for more than fifty years. They have two children, a son (Robert Tillman II, married to Annette) and a daughter (Melissa), and one grandson (Tobias Robert Stephen).

R. T. is a graduate of Trevecca Nazarene University (A.B.), Southern Baptist Theological Seminary (M.Div.), the University of Louisville (M.A.) and Oxford University (D.Phil.*Oxon.*). His doctoral thesis was published by Oxford University Press under the title *Calvin and English Calvinism to 1647*. He was awarded the D.D. by Trevecca Nazarene University in 2008.

Before he and his family went to England, R. T. pastored churches in Palmer, Tennessee; Carlisle, Ohio; Fort Lauderdale, Florida; and Salem, Indiana. He was pastor of Calvary Baptist Church in Lower Heyford, Oxfordshire, England (paralleling his three years at Oxford). He became the minister of Westminster Chapel on February 1, 1977, and was there for exactly 25 years, succeeding G. Campbell Morgan and D. Martyn Lloyd-Jones. He retired on February 1, 2002. His wrote about his 25 years at Westminster Chapel in his book *In Pursuit of His Glory*.

Shortly after Dr. Kendall's "retirement," he became involved in the Alexandria Peace Process, founded by Lord Carey, former Archbishop of Canterbury, and Canon Andrew White, the archbishop's envoy to the Middle East. From this came a special relationship with the late Yasser Arafat, president of the Palestinian National Authority, and Rabbi David Rosen, Israel's most distinguished orthodox Jewish rabbi. R. T. and David wrote a book together, *The Christian and the Pharisee*.

Dr. Kendall is the author of more than fifty books, including *Total Forgiveness*, *The Anointing*, *Sensitivity of the Spirit*, *The Parables of Jesus*, *God Meant It for Good* and *Did You Think to Pray?* He has an international ministry and spends his time preaching and writing. He and Louise currently live on Hickory Lake in Hendersonville, Tennessee, where he fishes occasionally.

More Insight from R. T. Kendall

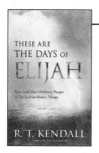
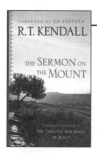
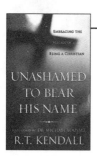